OTHER FARM JOURNAL CRAFT BOOKS

Knit Sweaters the Easy Way

Scrap Saver's Stitchery Book

More Scrap Saver's Stitchery

Let's Make a Patchwork Quilt

Farm Journal's Homespun Christmas

Farm Journal's Design-and-Sew Children's Clothes

Easy Sewing with Knits

Modern Patchwork

Patterns for Appliqué and Pieced Work

—and ways to use them

By Jean Gillies

FARM JOURNAL, INC.
Philadelphia, Pennsylvania

Distributed to the trade by
Doubleday & Company, Inc.
Garden City, New York

With special thanks to Regan Brown, Jessie MacDonald,
Carol Mankin and Jeannette Muir, all seasoned quilters,
who contributed their knowledge and skill in turning
out many of the samples shown in this book. Thanks,
also, to Ann Tomlinson, who graciously let the group
meet in her fabric shop to discuss various projects
along the way.

Book Design: Michael P. Durning
Photography: George Faraghan Studio
Illustrations: Len Epstein

Library of Congress Cataloging in Publication Data
Gillies, Jean.
    Patterns for appliqué and pieced work
    —and ways to use them.

    Includes index.
    1. Appliqué—Patterns.   2. Quilting—Patterns.
    3. Patchwork—Patterns.   I. Title
TT779.G54   1982   746.44'5041   82-12020
ISBN 0-385-18135-3

Contents

1
Guides for appliqué, pieced work and quilting

If you love to sew or quilt, but don't like to draw patterns, this book is for you. You'll find more than 50 full-size patterns to trace directly from the book, plus suggestions for putting them to use. There are directions for making pillows, tote bags, placemats, potholders, crib quilts and baby bibs—all background items for your appliqué and pieced work.

For easy projects, you can simply trace the patterns onto fabric and outline them with contrasting thread. Or use the patterns as quilting designs.

Many patterns are interchangeable. All finished blocks for pillows and tote bags are 14″ square, so they're easy to switch. You also can use the crib quilt patterns to decorate pillows or totes. (The basic crib quilt block is 12″ square, but the appliqués look just fine on larger blocks.)

If you want to use the Peeping Cat tote design for a crib quilt, the change works that way, too. And almost any block can be edged with bias binding or framed to become a wall hanging.

There are smaller designs for potholders and for clothing in

Chapters 5 and 7. These, too, are versatile. Use them in groups to fill a large block, or frame one with a fabric border, following directions for the Owl pillow on page 9.

Of course, you can show off larger designs on clothing, too. The Big Sun tote bag appliqué would be eye-catching on the back of a denim jacket, and the Little Bear crib quilt appliqué would work wonders on the front of a sweat shirt.

For fun, we made some designs double and stuffed them as ornaments. See Chapter 8 for miniatures, pincushions and soft sculptures.

This book gives you many patterns, with suggestions for different uses. Your imagination will generate even more uses as you begin to cut and stitch.

If you are an experienced sewer or quilter, you probably have your own favorite methods of working. If not, you can refer to the general directions that follow. There are suggestions for preparing fabric; a list of helpful supplies; guides for doing appliqué, pieced work, quilting and outlining; and directions for making a continuous strip of bias.

Preparing fabric

If you're going to make something that will be washed, don't cut the fabric until you test it for colorfastness and preshrink it. (Even if the bolt is labeled "preshrunk," the fabric could shrink a little more.) This ensures that your finished work can be washed with no problems—and you won't be afraid to sponge away an accidental spot while you're working.

Dunk each fabric piece in a separate bowl of hot water (use those plastic containers you've been saving), and leave it until the water is cool. If the water remains clear, put the fabric in the dryer or hang it up to dry.

If the color bleeds (runs), it may be a warning that the fabric will continue to bleed and ruin your finished project. But don't give up immediately—the problem may be excessive dye that will wash out. Change the water several times, then wash the fabric with detergent. After the fabric is dry, test it in water again. If the color still bleeds, eliminate that fabric.

The hot-water dunk followed by dryer-drying will preshrink

the fabric. However, you may want to wash and dry the fabric, following the same laundry methods you plan to use for the finished item.

Suggested supplies

Tracing paper: A roll of tracing paper is handy because you can cut off the size you need. However, you can tape together several sheets from a pad to make a bigger sheet.

Tagboard or similar weight material, such as a file folder: It should be firm enough to keep its shape as you trace around it, yet thin enough to give fabric a sharp edge when you press an appliqué over it.

Shears: Try to keep one pair for cutting fabrics and another pair for paper. It's also helpful to have a good pair of embroidery scissors with points that cut right to the tips—to slash close to stitching and into points.

Compass for drawing circles, *ruler, carbon paper* for tracing patterns onto tagboard, a *soft pencil* for marking light fabrics, and a *white dressmaker's pencil* for marking dark fabrics.

Open-toe presser foot if you use a zigzag machine for stitching appliqués or embroidery lines. This lets you see the lines you are stitching, which is difficult with a presser foot that is closed in front. (Of course, you don't need a machine that stitches zigzag to use this book. Everything can be done with straight machine stitching and/or hand sewing.)

Plus: It's nice to have a *dressmaker's square* or *T-square* for making square corners and marking quilt blocks.

General guides for appliqué

You can appliqué by hand or machine. Whichever method you choose, all the steps are given below.

For appliqué designs, use closely woven fabrics that won't fray easily. Otherwise, your work may quickly pull apart. For machine work, you'll have best results if you use firm, crisp fabrics, especially for the background. A soft, thin fabric may pucker when an appliqué is machine-stitched to it.

1. Trace pattern. Place tracing paper over appliqué pattern in book and trace complete design.

2. Make templates. Place tracing paper pattern over tagboard or material of similar weight, such as a file folder. Slip a sheet of carbon paper between, and retrace the pattern. Cut tagboard pattern apart to make a separate template for each piece of the design, and label pieces.

3. Prepare appliqués.

To appliqué by hand: Place template, right side up, on *right* side of fabric, and trace with a sharp pencil. Then position tracing paper pattern over outline and transfer inside design lines for embroidery or quilting by pressing pencil through paper to make a line of light dots. Remove paper and connect dots with light pencil lines. (On dark fabric, puncture paper with a sharp pencil, then mark with a white dressmaker's pencil.) Cut out fabric, adding a ¼" seam allowance.

Note: Most seam allowances will be turned to the wrong side. However, if a seam will be overlapped by another, it is left flat.

For seam allowances to be turned, machine-stitch along any inside curves and corners, just outside the pencil line (Fig. 1).

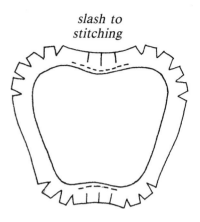

slash to stitching

Fig. 1 *Preparing fabric for hand appliqué*

Slash seam allowance to stitching; this will allow fabric to spread when it is turned to wrong side. On outside curves, cut out small V-shaped pieces to reduce bulk.

Turn seam allowance to wrong side. It may help to place template on wrong side of appliqué and press seam allowance over template. Roll any stitching on curves or corners to wrong side so it will not show. Trim seam allowance to under ¼".

Note: When a solid color overlaps a print (or a light color overlaps a darker color), the bottom fabric may show through. To prevent this, you can underline the appliqué with white fabric that is cut the same shape (with no seam allowance). Baste to back of appliqué.

Baste appliqué seam allowance to wrong side.

To appliqué by machine: For all pieces, press lightweight, fusible interfacing to wrong side of fabric. Place template, right side up, on *right* side of interfaced fabric, and trace with a sharp pencil. Then position tracing paper pattern over outline and transfer inside design lines for embroidery or quilting by pressing pencil through paper to make a line of light dots. Remove paper and connect dots with light pencil lines. (On dark fabric, puncture paper with a sharp pencil, then mark with a white dressmaker's pencil.)

For any seam to be covered by another appliqué piece, mark a 1/8″ seam allowance (under-lap); there are no other seam allowances unless noted. Cut out fabric.

4. Position appliqués. Most designs are centered. To find center of background fabric, fold fabric in half crosswise and lengthwise; press folds at center lightly with fingers.

To help position appliqués, place tracing paper pattern over background fabric and transfer appliqué placement lines. (For some designs, you can simply arrange the appliqué pieces under the tracing paper.) Pin appliqués in place and baste.

5. Stitch appliqués. If any pieces overlap, begin stitching on the bottom layer, and end with the top layer.

By hand: Use matching thread and an invisible hemming stitch (Fig. 2). If you want to outline the shape, you can attach the appliqué with a blanket stitch (Fig. 3), using two strands of embroidery floss in a contrasting color. Or, after the appliqué is stitched in place, outline the shape with a stem stitch (Fig. 4), using two strands of embroidery floss.

By machine: Use matching or contrasting thread and an open-toe presser foot. Set the machine for a satin zigzag stitch in

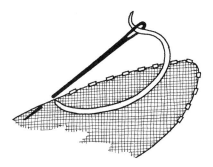

Fig. 2 *Hemming stitch for appliqué. Bring needle up from wrong side of fabric, catching folded edge of appliqué. Take a diagonal stitch, inserting needle close to where thread emerged; bring needle out 1/8″ ahead, through folded edge of appliqué.*

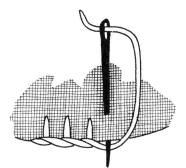

Fig. 3 *Blanket stitch. Work from left to right. Bring needle up from wrong side, just below edge of appliqué. Hold thread with thumb and insert needle vertically into appliqué; bring needle out under edge of appliqué and over thread. Keep stitches uniform in depth and evenly spaced.*

Fig. 4 *Stem stitch. Work from left to right. Take small back stitches, with each stitch overlapping the previous stitch. You can keep thread above or below needle, but be consistent.*

a medium-to-wide width, and loosen the top tension. For stitching appliqués to knitted fabrics, use a ballpoint machine needle.

To keep fabric smooth, stitch over a piece of typing paper or a special nonwoven stabilizer fabric that is sold in some fabric stores. After stitching, tear away the paper or stabilizer.

If machine appliqué is new to you, practice on scraps until you feel comfortable with it. Straight lines and gentle curves are easy, but it takes special know-how to keep lines smooth and stitches close together as

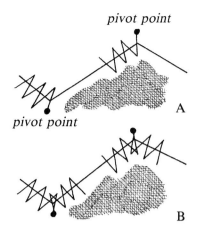

Fig. 5 *Pivoting at corners (machine stitching)*

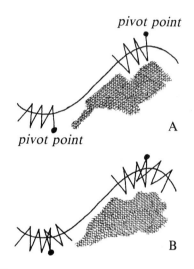

Fig. 6 *Pivoting on curves (machine stitching)*

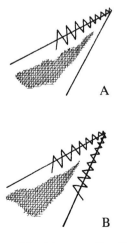

Fig. 7 *Machine-appliquéing a point*

you go around corners and sharp curves.

You have to pivot. To do this, stop stitching with needle still in the fabric. Lift the presser foot and pivot the fabric slightly, then continue stitching. At a corner, one pivot may do the job. On a sharp curve, you have to make several pivots to keep the line smooth.

Direction of the pivot depends on the direction of the corner or curve. For corners, see Fig. 5. For curves, see Fig. 6. After a pivot, stitches will overlap a bit.

For points, gradually decrease stitch width and pivot at the point. Reposition needle if necessary, and continue stitching, gradually increasing stitch width, as in Fig. 7.

6. Add embroidery lines.
Don't be afraid to mix machine work and handwork. You may find it easier to embroider small circles and curves by hand after you have appliquéd large shapes by machine.

By hand: Use two strands of embroidery floss for most work (more strands to make heavier lines). For straight lines, work a stem stitch (Fig. 4). For a wider line, add a second stem stitch or use the chain stitch (Fig. 8). For solid filled-in areas such as eyes, use the satin stitch (Fig. 9).

By machine: You can use a narrow-to-medium zigzag stitch for embroidery lines, and a wider satin stitch for filled-in areas such as eyes. Or you can use a straight stitch for lines, with regular or special topstitching thread in the top of the machine; stitch lines twice to make them heavier, if you wish.

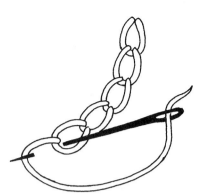

Fig. 8 *Chain stitch. Work from right to left. Bring needle up from wrong side, and hold thread against fabric with thumb. Insert needle close to where thread came out and take a stitch, bringing needle out over thread to form a loop. Continue, beginning the next stitch inside the loop to form a chain.*

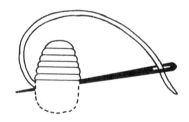

Fig. 9 *Satin stitch. Bring needle up on left side of design. Take a horizontal stitch, inserting needle on right side of design. Carry thread behind work, bringing needle up just under first stitch at left. Keep stitches parallel across the design and close together.*

General guides for pieced work

1. Trace pattern. Place tracing paper over pattern pieces in book and trace.

2. Make a template for each piece. Place tracing paper pattern over tagboard or material of similar weight, such as a file folder. Slip a sheet of carbon paper between, and retrace pattern pieces. Cut out templates and label.

3. Mark and cut fabric. Trace templates, right side down, on *wrong* side of fabric, using a pencil to mark the exact seam line for stitching. Take care in marking corners—this helps you to match points exactly.

Cut fabric, adding a ¼ " seam allowance (½ " if making a pillow, tote bag or placemat).

4. Join pieces. Lay fabric pieces flat, right side up, to form design. Pin pieces, right sides together, along seam (pencil) lines, being careful to match seam ends. By machine, stitch from raw edge to raw edge, unless otherwise noted (points are one exception).

Press seam allowances to one side (do not press open), and trim to just under ¼ ". Try to press seams to the darker fabric. When two finished seams are joined, try to have the seam allowances pressed in opposite directions to distribute bulk.

General guides for quilting

1. Mark fabric with any quilting lines that may be needed, using a pencil. For simple quilting, no marking is necessary; you can follow seam lines as a guide (see Step 3).

2. Stack the layers. Arrange in this order: backing fabric, right side down; batting; finished block (or quilt), right side up. Baste layers together to keep them from shifting, sewing from center of block (or quilt) to outside.

Note: To hand-quilt within an appliqué, it often helps to eliminate the layer of background fabric beneath it. To do this, carefully cut away the background fabric under the appliqué, leaving a seam allowance just under ¼ ". Do this before block is stacked over batting for quilting.

3. Quilt in any pattern you wish, using matching or contrasting thread.

For pieced work: As a general guide, quilt inside all pieces, ¼ " from seam lines. Or you can quilt just solid color areas where your work will show, making the non-quilted areas pop out. If you want to add extra quilting, work a design in the solid areas. (Transfer the design to the block before stacking over batting.)

For appliqués: Quilt around the design. Repeat the same lines, radiating out from the appliqué. On some designs, you may wish to quilt within the appliqué, sewing directly over seam lines, or ¼ " from them.

Quilting by hand: Sew with short needles called Betweens. Use quilting thread, or substitute regular thread that you've waxed to keep it from tangling. (Beeswax is sold with sewing supplies.) For large projects such as a crib quilt, you may want to use a quilting hoop.

Begin quilting by burying the knot in the batting (pull it through the backing fabric). Use a small, even running stitch (Fig. 10), going through all lay-

Fig. 10 *Running stitch. Work from right to left, making small even stitches.*

ers with each stitch. To end stitching, make a knot in the thread, close to the fabric. Take one more stitch, pulling the knot through the top fabric and into the batting; bring needle up along the line yet to be quilted. Clip thread close to fabric.

Quilting by machine: Use regular thread and a medium-to-long straight stitch. Practice on layers of fabric the same thickness as the quilt block.

General guides for outlining designs

Outlining is a good technique for quick projects. Just transfer pattern lines to background fabric and go over the lines with machine stitching, hand embroidery or quilting.

1. Trace pattern from book onto tracing paper, following any special directions for the individual design.

2. Cut background fabric (front) to size for pillow, tote bag, potholder or other item.

3. Transfer pattern by positioning tracing paper pattern over right side of background fabric and pressing a sharp pencil through paper to make a line of light dots. Remove paper and connect dots with light pencil lines. (On dark fabric, puncture paper with a sharp pencil, then mark with a white dressmaker's pencil.)

4. Outline design. Stitch on the single layer of fabric by hand or machine, following Step 6 (*Add embroidery lines* under *General guides for appliqué*), page 5.

Or, ready block for quilting and quilt the design by hand or machine; see *General guides for quilting*, page 5.

Making a continuous bias strip

Bias binding is available in a range of standard colors and sizes, but you may not be able to find what you want. In that case, you can make your own bias—to bind a potholder or crib quilt, or to cover cable cord for a pillow edge.

It's best to mark the fabric for bias first, then use the remaining fabric for cutting appliqué and pieced work patterns.

1. Mark the true bias (45° angle to the selvage) with a pen-

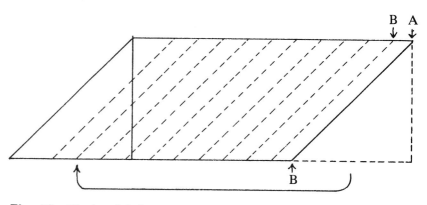

Fig. 12 *Piecing fabric to get maximum length of bias*

cil on the wrong side of fabric. From this line, measure the strips (Fig. 11).

As a general rule, use ¼ yard of fabric for potholder binding; measure 3 strips, each 1″ wide, to yield a yard of bias.

To cover cable cord for a pillow, use ½ yard of fabric; measure four strips, each 1″ wide, to yield two yards of bias. (You could use only ¼ yard and cut more strips to cover the cord, but that would require more seam joinings.)

For crib quilt binding, use ½ yard of fabric. On wrong side, mark the first line of bias, then cut away the resulting triangle (Fig. 12). Move triangle to left side of fabric, and machine-stitch the straight edges, right sides together. Mark 10 strips, each 3″ wide, to yield six yards of bias.

2. Make tube. Cut along outside pencil lines (one line of crib quilt bias has already been cut). Join the two straight edges, right sides together, to form a tube (Fig. 13). Arrange pencil lines, beginning with the B points, so they match ¼″ from the edge where seam will be stitched. One width of bias will extend beyond the tube at each

end. Stitch a ¼″ seam and press it open.

3. Cut and press. Begin cutting the tube at one end and continue until tube becomes one continuous bias strip.

For double-fold bias (potholder and quilt binding), fold bias in half lengthwise, right side out, and press (do not stretch). Open fabric, and fold each raw edge to center of wrong side; press. Refold lengthwise and press.

To cover cable cord for a pillow, see page 8.

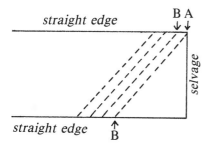

Fig. 11 *Marking bias strips*

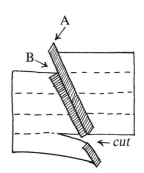

Fig. 13 *Joining straight edges to form a tube*

2

Pillows

Toss a few pillows on the sofa, a few on each bed, and maybe one or two on the floor. There's always room for one more.

Here are eight pillow top designs to tempt you. There's a mix of appliqué and pieced work, plus complete directions for finishing a pillow.

For more choices, look at the tote bag designs in Chapter 3. They're interchangeable—each pillow top and tote front is 14" square when finished. For example, see the Big Sun tote pattern quilted on a pillow, page 120.

You also could make a pillow using one of the crib quilt patterns from Chapter 6. Any of the potholder appliqués in Chapter 5 can be stitched on the Owl pillow (instead of the owl)—that center square is just the right size. Even the placemat patterns in Chapter 4 can be used for pillows. So when you finish making pillows for yourself, you can stitch special gifts for friends.

There are choices for finishing the pillow edge. Leave it plain, or add a trim—cording or ruffle, purchased or custom-made.

There are choices for finishing the back, too. Sew on a one-piece square, or make a back with an opening (envelope style or zipper) so you can remove the cover for cleaning.

You can even make a larger pillow—maybe 16" square, for example. Just enlarge the background block or add a 1" border. (If the pattern already has a border, make it 1" wider.) Increase measurements accordingly for batting, backing and pillow back.

You'll find materials needed and special instructions under the heading for each design. Then follow the general directions for making a pillow.

To make a pillow

Dimensions given are for a 14"-square pillow.

1. Complete pillow top
(front), following directions for pattern you choose. Machine-stitch around edge, directly over seam (pencil) line.

2. Quilt the block.
Mark any needed quilting lines. Then stack layers in this order: muslin (or other backing fabric); batting; pillow front, right side up. Baste layers together and quilt as desired. (See *General guides for quilting,* page 5.)

If no cording or ruffle is to be added (Step 3), baste around edge, directly over stitching on pillow front.

3. Add ruffle or cording
(optional).

Purchased ruffle or cording: Leave a 2" length (or tail) of ruffle or cording free, and begin pinning trim to bottom edge of block so joining will be centered. Have finished edge of trim toward center of block (see Fig. 1). Stitching on trim should be directly over stitching at edge of block.

Gently round corners. On ruffle, allow extra fullness. On cording, slash seam allowance to stitching so cording can spread (Fig. 1). Baste trim around block to where joining will be made.

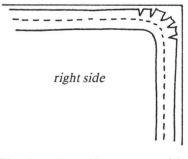

right side

Fig. 1   *Rounding corner with cording*

To join purchased ruffle, make a French seam so there is no raw edge. First stitch a ⅛" seam with wrong sides of ruffle together. Turn fabric so right sides are together, folding along stitched seam; stitch a ¼" seam. Machine-stitch ruffle to block.

To join cording, open stitching for 1" on the 2" tail. Clip off ¾" of cord, and fold raw fabric edge ¼" to wrong side. Cut other end of cording so it will butt against clipped cord, and lay it (still covered) inside opened fabric (Fig. 2). Hand-stitch joinings in place. Then machine-stitch cording to block.

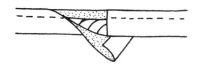

Fig. 2 *Joining cording*

To make your own cording: First make a continuous strip of bias (see page 6). Fold the bias, right side out, over purchased cable cord, and machine-stitch close to cord with zipper foot (Fig. 3).

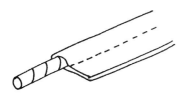

Fig. 3 *Covering cord*

Custom-made ruffle: A double ruffle 3" wide and about 2½ times the circumference of the block edge makes an attractive finish. From 1¼ yard of 44"-wide fabric, you can make a double ruffle, cut a pillow back, and have fabric for the front block (background for appliqué or fabric for a pieced design).

To help measure the ruffle, make a template 6½" wide and about 10" long.

On wrong side of fabric, mark three 6½"-wide rows across fabric, following cross-wise grain. On a fourth row, mark 10" across. Cut fabric on pencil lines and cut off selvages.

Pin ends of ruffle pieces, right sides together, to form a ring. Machine-stitch ¼" seams, and press open.

To form a double ruffle, fold ring in half; have right side out and raw edges together. Press.

Fold ring into fourths and mark quarter points with a straight line in the seam allowance. Fold again into eighths and mark points with an X.

Machine-gather ruffle ¼" from the raw edge, using a strong thread in the bobbin (heavy duty or topstitching thread). Stitch each quarter section separately, overlapping areas.

Gather ruffle, one section at a time, by pulling bobbin thread at each end of the stitching. Carefully work fullness to center (X mark).

Pin ruffle to right side of block, with gathering line directly over stitching at edge of block, and folded edge of ruffle toward center of block. Place a quarter mark at each corner, and center an X mark on each side. Distribute fullness, adding extra at corners.

By hand, baste ruffle to block, lining up stitches on ruffle with stitched line on block. Check corners to be sure ruffle is full enough. Machine-stitch ruffle in place. Remove any gatherings that show.

4. Add pillow back to complete the pillow cover. Choose one of

these three ways.

One-piece back with no opening: Cut a 15" square of fabric and machine-stitch it to the pillow front, right sides together. Make a ½" seam, leaving 8" open for turning. Trim batting and backing to stitching; clip fabric across corners. Turn to right side, and work seam to edge. Stuff with fiberfill and close opening by hand.

Envelope closure, with two overlapping sections: Cut two pieces of fabric, each 10½x15". On one long edge of each piece, make a double hem, ¼" each turn.

Place back pieces on top of front, right sides together, with hemmed edges of back overlapping horizontally at center (Fig. 4). Pin in a few places to hold.

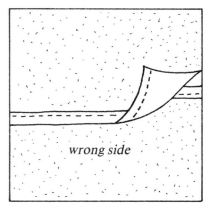

wrong side

Fig. 4 *Envelope back*

Turn layers over so front is on top. Pin edges together. Machine-stitch directly over stitched line at edge. Trim batting and backing to stitching; clip fabric across corners.

Turn to right side, and work seam to edge. Make inner pillow (see Step 5).

Hidden zipper closure: Cut a piece of fabric 3½x15" for upper back. Press the bottom (long) edge 1" to the wrong side.

Cut a second piece of fabric, 13¼x15″, for lower back. Press the top (long) edge ¼″ to the wrong side.

Position the zipper and lower back right side up. Center the turned edge of lower back over zipper; have fold close to the zipper teeth. Use a zipper foot to topstitch fabric to zipper tape. Open zipper and restitch closer to teeth at opening.

Lay upper back flat, wrong side up, with folded edge at bottom. On top of this, place lower back with zipper, wrong side up; have top (free) edge of zipper running along top (raw) edge of fold; baste zipper to fabric.

Turn to right side and check basting to be sure it is straight. Topstitch along basted line. Then baste and topstitch along folded edge, 1″ in from each raw edge.

Open zipper. Pin back to front, right sides together, with pins perpendicular to edges.

Turn layers over, so wrong side of front is on top. Machine-stitch together, sewing directly over stitched line along edge. Trim batting and backing to stitching; clip fabric across corners.

Turn to right side, and work seam to edge. Make inner pillow (see Step 5).

5. Make inner pillow (for removable pillow cover). Use the two squares of 15x15″ muslin and the two squares of 15x15″ batting.

Stack layers in this order: batting (2 layers); fabric (2 layers), with right sides together. Stitch together, ½″ from edge, leaving 8″ open for turning. Cut across corners to trim.

Turn to right side. Stuff center by adding fiberfill *between* the layers of batting (batting helps keep outside of pillow smooth). Close opening with hand stitches.

Put inner pillow into finished pillow cover and close opening.

OWL

Fig. 5 Owl
(color photo, page 12)

This appliqué owl pattern would fit a potholder, and any of the potholder appliqués in Chapter 5 could be substituted for the owl. The center block is sized to display them all.

Materials

½ yd. yellow-gold print, 44″
  wide, for border and back
yellow-gold fabric, 7x7″
bright green fabric, 8½x8½″,
  plus scrap for two inner eye
  circles
lightweight, fusible interfacing,
  7x8″ (for machine appliqué)
polyester batting, 15x15″
muslin or similar fabric, 15x15″,
  for backing
polyester fiberfill
thread for stitching and quilting
black embroidery floss or
  thread, for embroidery lines
yellow zipper, 12″ (optional)
for inner pillow (optional):
  2 squares polyester batting
  and 2 squares muslin or
  similar fabric, 15x15″ each

Directions

See *General guides for appliqué*, page 2.

1. Trace Owl and border patterns, page 18. Make templates for owl, inner eye circle and full border piece.
2. On *wrong* side of yellow-gold print fabric, trace four full border pieces. Cut out, adding a ½″ seam allowance.
3. Prepare and cut appliqué pieces for either hand or machine stitching. Use yellow-gold for owl, and bright green for two inner eye circles.
4. Center owl on right side of green square, and sew in place. Position inner green eyes and sew in place.
5. Add embroidery lines in black.
6. Join border pieces at corners; begin stitching at outside edge, and stop exactly at end of seam (pencil) line at inner edge. Press seams open.
7. Press inner edge of border to wrong side along seam line. Position border over green square.

   Work on one side at a time. Lift border to expose seam allowances. Pin border to green fabric (raw edges should be even if you have cut ½″ seam allowances). Machine-stitch ½″ seams.
8. Quilt and finish pillow; see *To make a pillow*, page 7.

CLAMSHELL FLOWER

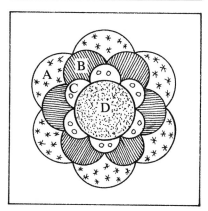

Fig. 6 Clamshell Flower
(color photo, page 13)

Three rows of graduated clamshell shapes form this flower. A line of quilting inside the center circle and outside each ring of petals emphasizes the design.

Materials

½ yd. off-white fabric, 44″
wide, for front and back
rust print, 8x17″
beige print, 8½x11″
rust fabric with small white
dots, 6x11″
beige fabric with small dots,
6x6″
⅝ yd. lightweight, fusible inter-
facing, 22″ wide (for machine
appliqué)
polyester batting, 15x15″
muslin or similar fabric, 15x15″,
for backing
polyester fiberfill
thread for stitching and quilting
2 yd. rust cording (optional)
off-white zipper, 12″ (optional)
for inner pillow (optional):
2 squares polyester batting
and 2 squares muslin or
similar fabric, 15x15″ each

Directions

See *General guides for appliqué*, page 2.
1. Trace pattern pieces A-D for Clamshell Flower, page 19.

Make a template for each piece.
2. On *wrong* side of off-white fabric, mark a 14″ square for front block of pillow. Cut out, adding a ½″ seam allowance.
3. Prepare and cut appliqué pieces for either hand or machine stitching. Use rust print for six A pieces, beige print for six B pieces, rust with small dot for six C pieces, and beige with dot for one D piece.
4. Position appliqué pieces on right side of front block, forming design in Fig. 6. Sew in place.
5. Quilt block and finish pillow; see *To make a pillow*, page 7.

WALKING ROOSTER

Fig. 7 Walking Rooster
(color photo, page 13)

Black thread adds a strong outline to this determined-looking bird.

Materials

½ yd. off-white fabric, 44″
wide, for pillow front and
back
black print, 10x12″
red print, 8x10″
red fabric, 4x5½″
yellow fabric, 5x5″
½ yd. lightweight, fusible inter-
facing, 22″ wide (for machine
appliqué)
polyester batting, 15x15″
muslin or similar fabric, 15x15″,
for backing
polyester fiberfill
thread for stitching (use black
for machine appliqué) and
quilting
black embroidery floss (for
outlining hand appliqué)
2 yd. black cording (optional)
off-white zipper, 12″ (optional)
for inner pillow (optional):
2 squares polyester batting
and 2 squares muslin or
similar fabric, 15x15″ each

Directions

See *General guides for appliqué*, page 2.
1. Trace Walking Rooster pattern, pages 20-21. Make a template for each piece, A-I.
2. On *wrong* side of off-white fabric, mark a 14″ square for front block of pillow. Cut out, adding a ½″ seam allowance.
3. Prepare and cut appliqué pieces for either hand or machine stitching. Use black print for one A and one C; red print for one B and one D; red for one E; and yellow for one F (eye circle), one G (beak), one H and one I (legs).
4. Center appliqué pieces on right side of front block, and sew in place.
5. Add embroidery lines. Stitch eye in black.
6. Quilt block and finish pillow; see *To make a pillow*, page 7.

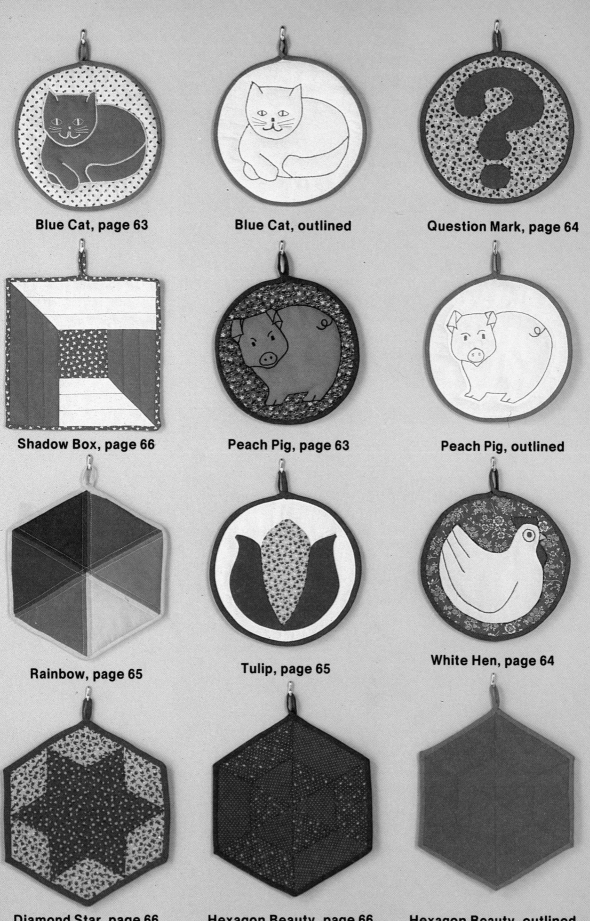

Blue Cat, page 63

Blue Cat, outlined

Question Mark, page 64

Shadow Box, page 66

Peach Pig, page 63

Peach Pig, outlined

Rainbow, page 65

Tulip, page 65

White Hen, page 64

Diamond Star, page 66

Hexagon Beauty, page 66

Hexagon Beauty, outlined

Pick one of these potholder patterns, then follow directions in Chapter 5 for making it.

Pillows offer an easy way to add color and interest to a room, and Chapter 2 gives complete directions for making these eight different designs. Top row, left to right, are the Owl (page 9), Magnolia Bud (page 15), Wheel of Destiny (page 17) and Clamshell Flower (page 10). Bottom row, left to right, are the Fruit Bowl (page 15), Twin Darts (page 16), Walking Rooster (page 10) and Star Rings (page 16).

Apple, page 96

Cherries, page 96

Bird, page 96

Aqua Dog, page 97

Let appliqués give clothing a custom-made look.

Chick, page 96

Dog with Butterfly, page 97

Duck, page 97

FRUIT BOWL

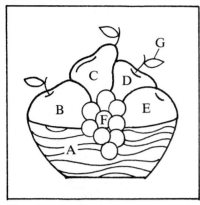

Fig. 8   Fruit Bowl
(color photo, page 12)

Colorful fabrics make this pillow a bright accent for your sofa. Each grape is outlined with white stitches. The highlight curve on the pear is green, and the stems and other design lines are black.

Materials

½ yd. white fabric, 44″ wide, for pillow front and back
blue print, 6x12″
red fabric, 4x5″
yellow-gold fabric, 4½x5½″
green fabric, 5x6″
orange fabric, 4x5″
purple fabric, 5x6″
⅜ yd. lightweight, fusible interfacing, 22″ wide (for machine appliqué)
polyester batting, 15x15″
muslin or similar fabric, 15x15″
polyester fiberfill
thread for stitching and quilting
white, green and black embroidery floss or thread, for embroidery lines
2 yd. blue cording (optional)
white zipper, 12″ (optional)
for inner pillow (optional):
*   2 squares polyester batting and 2 squares muslin or similar fabric, 15x15″ each*

Directions

See *General guides for appliqué work*, page 2.

1. Trace Fruit Bowl pattern, pages 22-23. Make a separate template for each piece, A-G. (Cut bunch of grapes F as one piece.)
2. On *wrong* side of white fabric, mark a 14″ square for front block of pillow. Cut out, adding a ½″ seam allowance.
3. Prepare and cut appliqué pieces for either hand or machine stitching. Use blue print for one A, red for one B, yellow-gold for one C, green for one D and three G pieces, orange for one E, and purple for one F.
4. Center appliqué pieces on right side of front block, and sew in place. For hand appliqué, use matching thread (outlining is done later). For machine appliqué, use white thread for grapes (including design lines), and matching thread for all other pieces.
5. Add embroidery lines. Use white to outline grapes. (A chain stitch with two strands of embroidery floss was used to hand-embroider sample pillow.) Use green for line on pear, black for stems and other lines.
6. Quilt block and finish pillow; see *To make a pillow*, page 7.

MAGNOLIA BUD

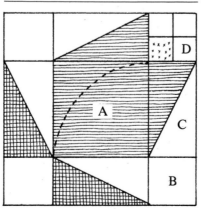

Fig. 9   Magnolia Bud
(color photo, page 12)

This spectacular flower shape has an Art Nouveau look. A curved line of quilting adds a petal shape, and bright pink cording frames the block.

Materials

½ yd. white fabric, 44″ wide, for design and back
bright pink fabric, 9x18″
green fabric, 9x9″
light pink scrap, for center of bud
polyester batting, 15x15″
muslin or similar fabric, 15x15″, for backing
polyester fiberfill
thread for stitching and quilting
2 yd. bright pink cording (optional)
white zipper, 12″ (optional)
for inner pillow (optional):
*   2 squares polyester batting and 2 squares muslin or similar fabric, 15x15″ each*

Directions

See *General guides for pieced work*, page 5.

1. Trace pattern pieces A-D for Magnolia Bud, page 24. Make a template for each piece.
2. Place templates on *wrong* side of fabric. On white, trace three B, two C, two C-reversed, and three D pieces. On bright pink, trace one A, one C and one C-reversed. On green, trace one C and one C-reversed. On light pink, trace one D. Cut out, adding a ½″ seam allowance.
3. Lay pieces flat, right side up, to form design in Fig. 9. Join pieces to form three rows. Then join rows to form the block.
4. Quilt block and finish pillow; see *To make a pillow*, page 7. Add a curved line of quilting on the center A piece to form a petal shape (see Fig. 9).

STAR RINGS

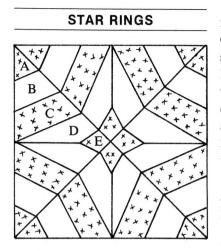

Fig. 10 Star Rings
(color photo, page 13)

This block forms an interesting overall pattern when it is repeated in a quilt without sashing. For our single-block pillow, we added a ruffle.

Take time to mark seam allowances (copy symbols from pattern) so you can keep pieces in order when joining them.

Materials

½ yd. green print, 44″ wide, for design and back (or 1¼ yd. if you also want a ruffle)
¼ yd. green fabric
polyester batting, 15x15″
muslin or similar fabric, 15x15″, for backing
polyester fiberfill
thread for stitching and quilting
green zipper, 12″ (optional)
for inner pillow (optional):
    2 squares polyester batting and 2 squares muslin or similar fabric, 15x15″ each

Directions

See *General guides for pieced work*, page 5.
1. Trace pattern pieces A-E for Star Rings, page 25. Make a template for each piece.
2. Place templates on *wrong* side of fabric. On print, trace

four A, four A-reversed, four C, four C-reversed, four E. On solid green, trace four B, four B-reversed, four D, four D-reversed. Label each piece, and copy edge markings. Cut out, adding a ½″ seam allowance.
3. Lay pieces flat, right side up, to form design in Fig. 10.

Make a unit by joining together an A, B, C and D. Repeat to make second unit (Fig. 11). To join the two units, sew the D pieces together. Begin stitching at the outside edge of block, and end exactly on the seam (pencil) line at center of design.

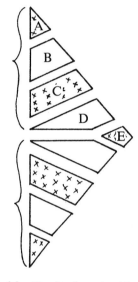

Fig. 11 *Beginning the block*

Add E to make a triangle. (You may want to do this stitching by hand to keep the point exact.)
Repeat steps to make three more triangles, and join the triangles to complete the block.
4. Quilt block and finish pillow; see *To make a pillow*, page 7.

TWIN DARTS

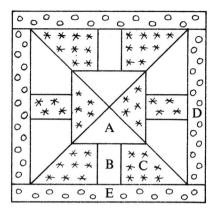

Fig. 12 Twin Darts
(color photo, page 12)

The 10″-square center of this pieced block has a 2″ border that matches the pillow back.

Materials

½ yd. brown print, 44″ wide, for border and back
beige print, 9x16″
orange fabric, 9x16″
polyester batting, 15x15″
muslin or similar fabric, 15x15″, for backing
polyester fiberfill
thread for stitching and quilting
brown zipper, 12″ (optional)
for inner pillow (optional):
    2 squares polyester batting and 2 squares muslin or similar fabric, 15x15″ each

Directions

See *General guides for pieced work*, page 5.
1. Trace pattern pieces A-E for Twin Darts, page 26. Make a template for each piece.
2. Place templates on *wrong* side of fabric. On both beige print and orange, trace two A, two B, two C and two C-reversed pieces. On brown print, trace two D and two E pieces. Cut out, adding a ½″ seam allowance.

3. Lay pieces flat, right side up, to form design in Fig. 12.

Work on one fourth of the center design (Fig. 13). Join the C-B-C pieces, and add an A to form a large triangle.

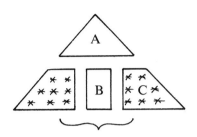

Fig. 13 *Forming a large triangle*

Repeat to make three more triangles, then join the triangles to form the design.

Add a D to each side. Add an E to top and bottom to complete the block.

4. Quilt block and finish pillow; see *To make a pillow*, page 7.

WHEEL OF DESTINY

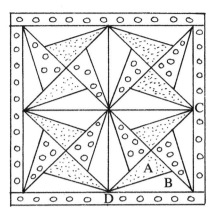

Fig. 14 Wheel of Destiny *(color photo, page 13)*

The basic design (with only two pattern pieces) is repeated four times. Then it's framed with a 1″ border. Areas of solid color invite some fancy quilting, and a quilting pattern is included.

Materials
½ yd. purple print, 44″ wide, for design, border and back
purple fabric with small white dots, 8x14″
¼ yd. turquoise fabric, 44″ wide
polyester batting, 15x15″
muslin or similar fabric, 15x15″, for backing
polyester fiberfill
thread for stitching and quilting
purple zipper, 12″ (optional)
for inner pillow (optional):
   2 squares polyester batting and 2 squares muslin or similar fabric, 15x15″ each

Directions
See *General guides for pieced work*, page 5.
1. Trace pattern pieces A-D for Wheel of Destiny, page 27. Make a template for each piece.
2. Place templates on *wrong* side of fabric. On purple print, trace two C and two D pieces.

On both purple print and purple with dot, trace four A and four A-reversed pieces. On turquoise, trace eight B and eight B-reversed pieces.

3. Lay pieces flat, right side up, to form design in Fig. 14. To make each small square, first stitch A pieces to B pieces to form triangles (Fig. 15). Join

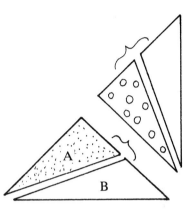

Fig. 15 *Forming triangles*

pairs of triangles to form half a square. Then join the two halves.

Join the four squares to form the center design. Add a C to each side. Add a D to top and bottom.

4. Quilt block and finish pillow; see *To make a pillow*, page 7.

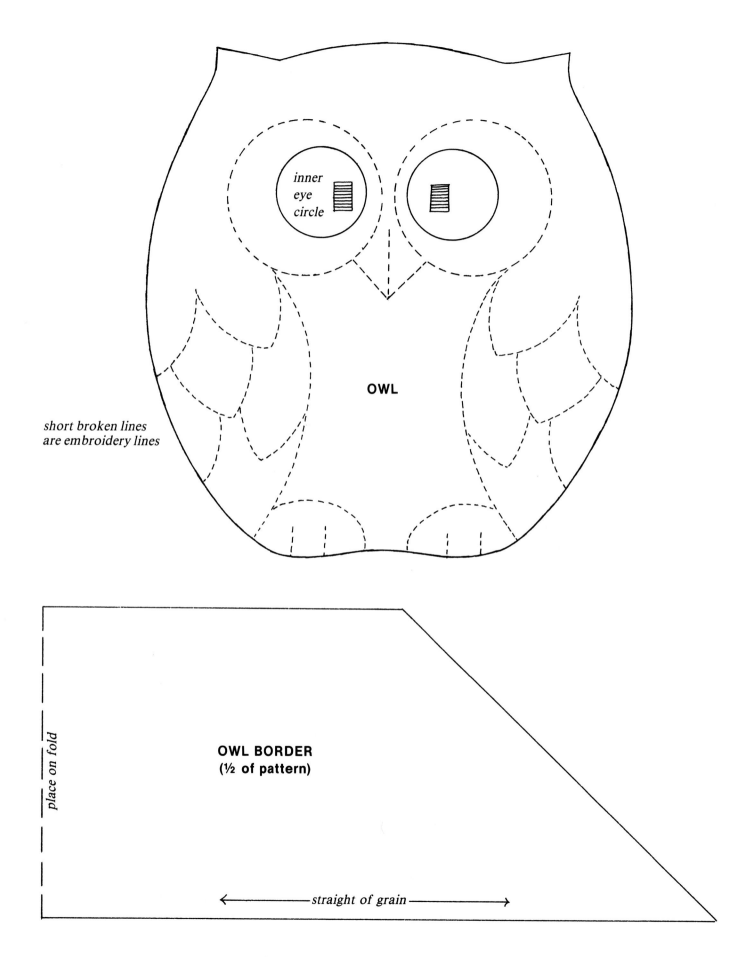

inner eye circle

OWL

short broken lines are embroidery lines

place on fold

**OWL BORDER
(½ of pattern)**

←——————— *straight of grain* ———————→

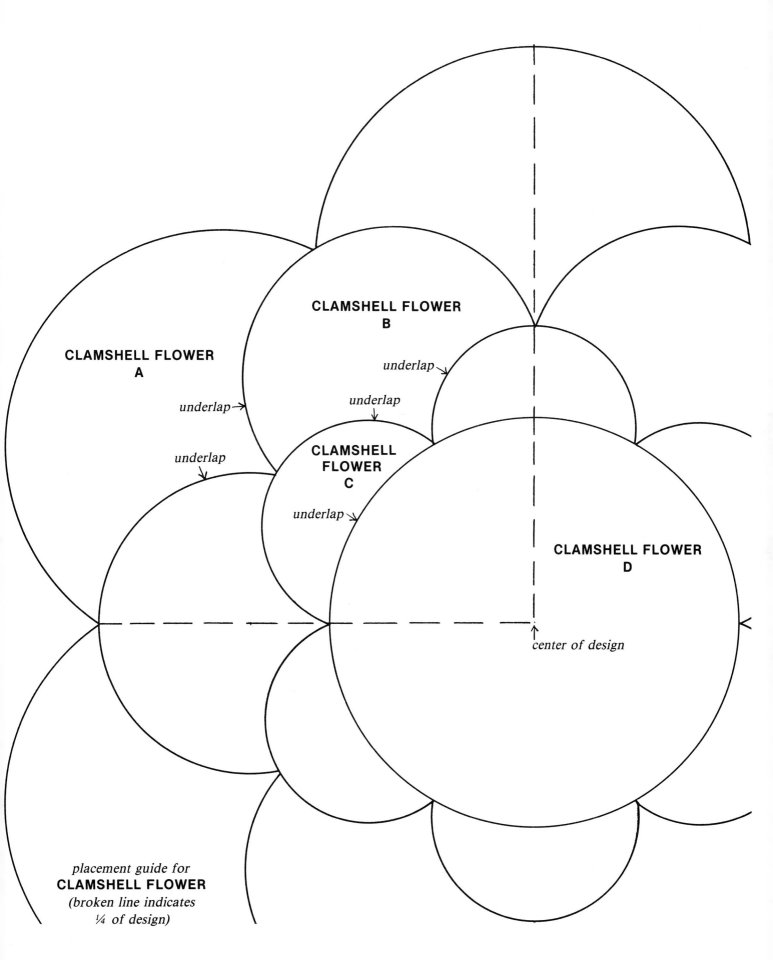

CLAMSHELL FLOWER
A

CLAMSHELL FLOWER
B

underlap →

underlap

underlap →

underlap

CLAMSHELL
FLOWER
C

underlap ↘

CLAMSHELL FLOWER
D

↑
center of design

placement guide for
CLAMSHELL FLOWER
*(broken line indicates
¼ of design)*

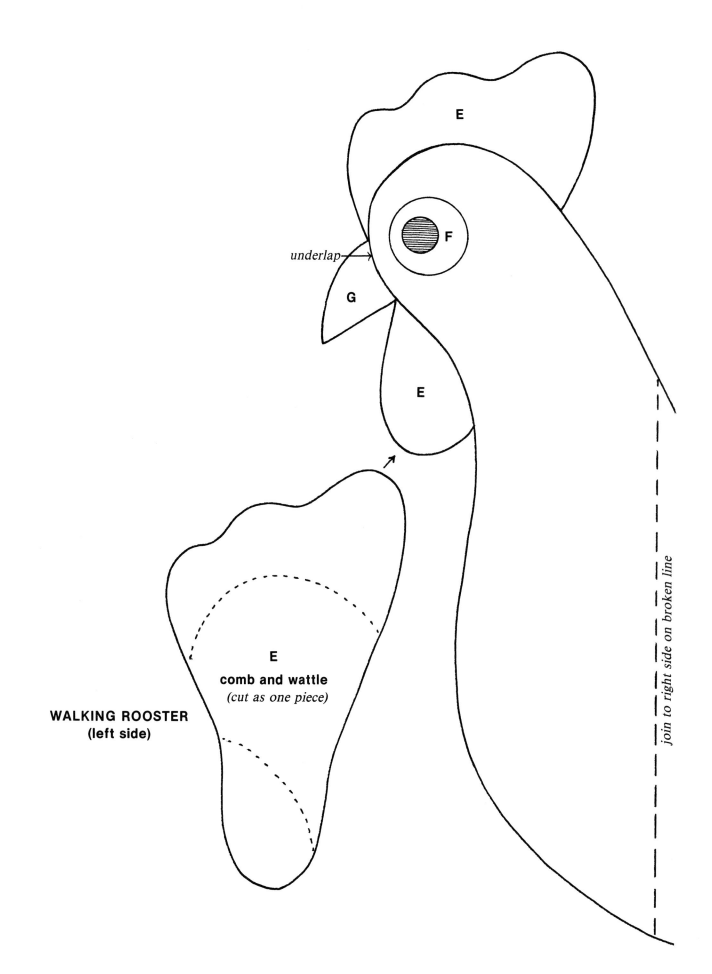

E

F

underlap→

G

E

E
comb and wattle
(cut as one piece)

WALKING ROOSTER
(left side)

join to right side on broken line

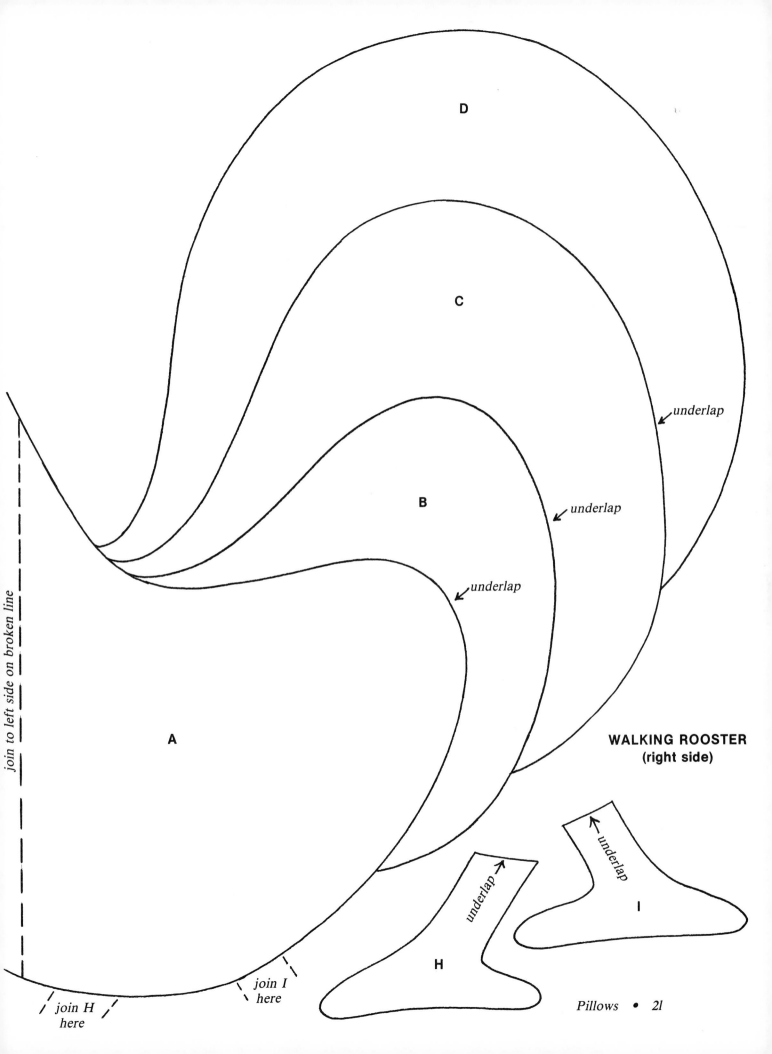

D

C

B

A

underlap

underlap

underlap

join to left side on broken line

**WALKING ROOSTER
(right side)**

underlap

underlap

I

H

*join I
here*

*join H
here*

Pillows • 2l

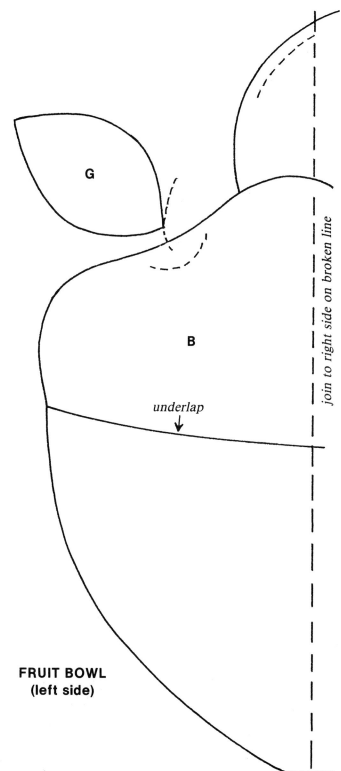

G

B

underlap
↓

join to right side on broken line

FRUIT BOWL
(left side)

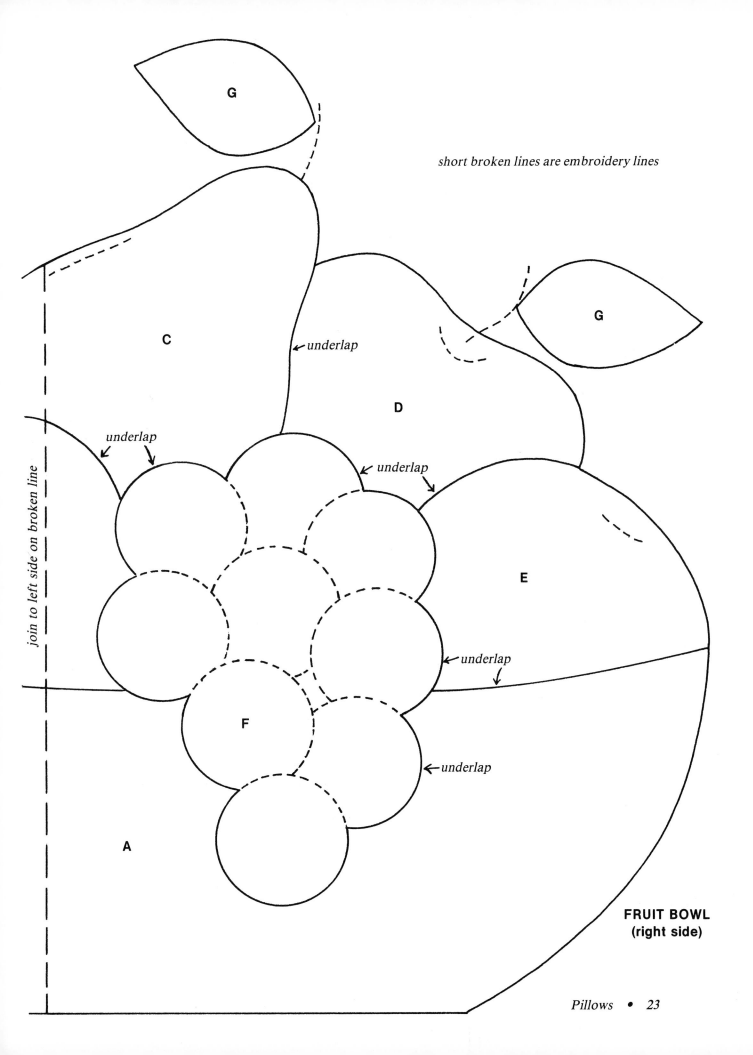

G

short broken lines are embroidery lines

C

← *underlap*

underlap

D

← *underlap*

join to left side on broken line

G

E

← *underlap*

← *underlap*

F

← *underlap*

A

FRUIT BOWL
(right side)

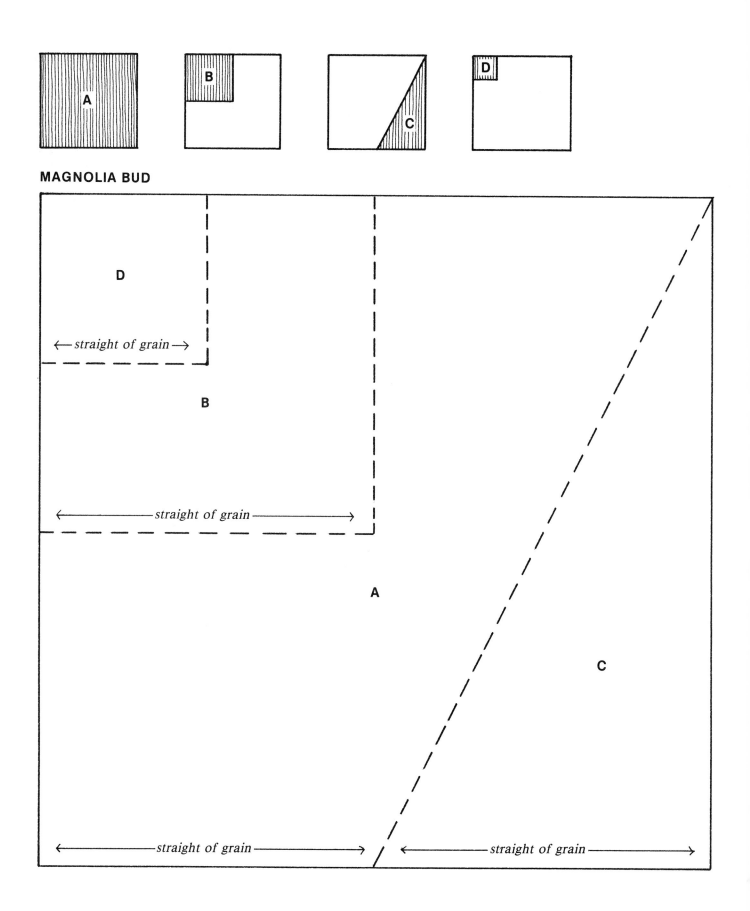

MAGNOLIA BUD

D

← straight of grain →

B

← straight of grain →

A

C

← straight of grain → ← straight of grain →

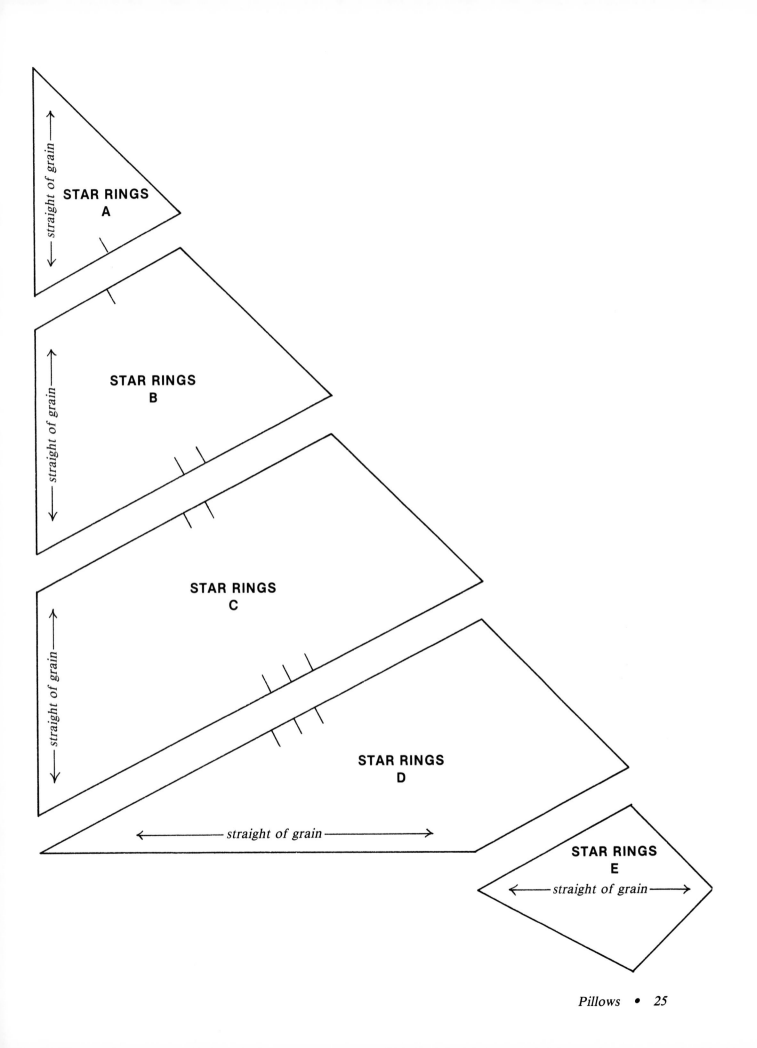

STAR RINGS
A

↑
straight of grain
↓

STAR RINGS
B

↑
straight of grain
↓

STAR RINGS
C

↑
straight of grain
↓

STAR RINGS
D

← straight of grain →

STAR RINGS
E

← straight of grain →

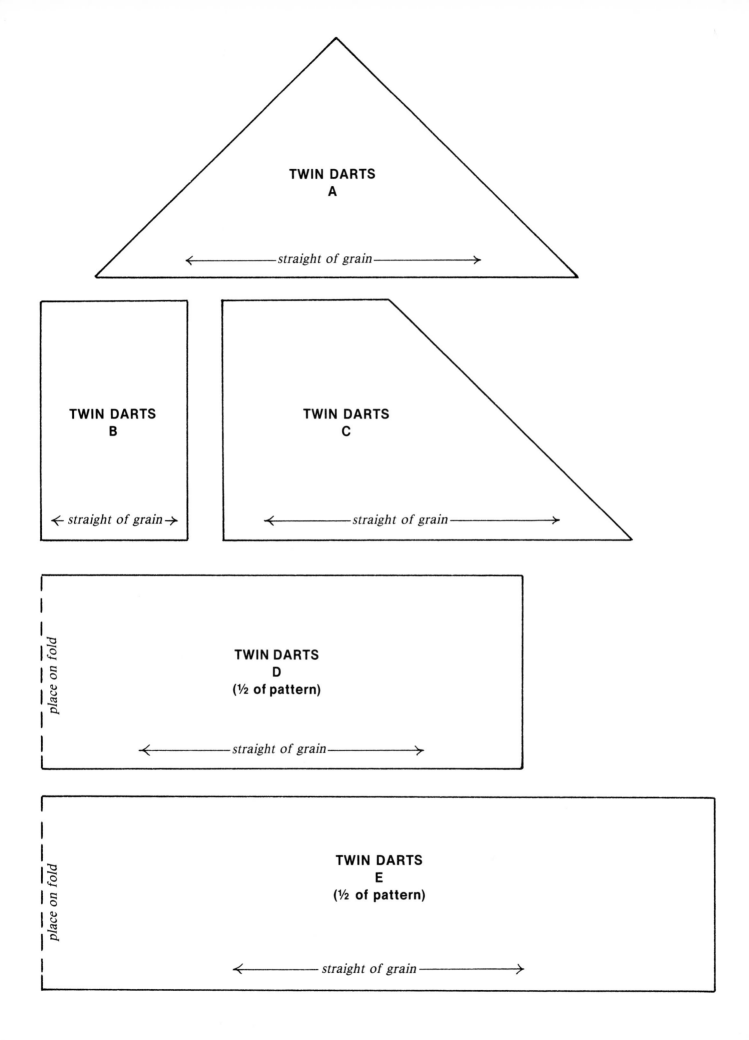

TWIN DARTS
A

← straight of grain →

TWIN DARTS
B

← straight of grain →

TWIN DARTS
C

← straight of grain →

place on fold

TWIN DARTS
D
(½ of pattern)

← straight of grain →

place on fold

TWIN DARTS
E
(½ of pattern)

← straight of grain →

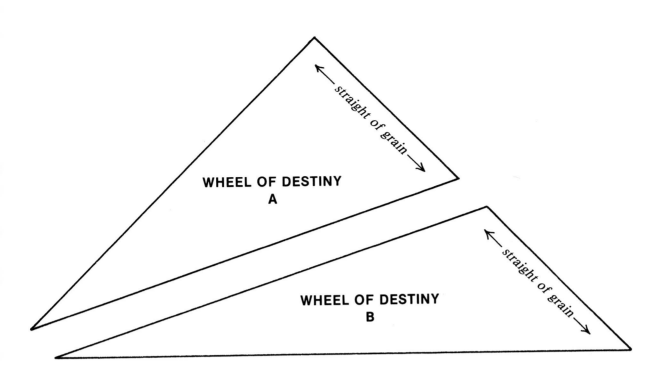

**WHEEL OF DESTINY
A**

straight of grain

**WHEEL OF DESTINY
B**

straight of grain

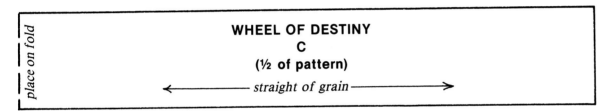

place on fold

**WHEEL OF DESTINY
C
(½ of pattern)**

←————— straight of grain —————→

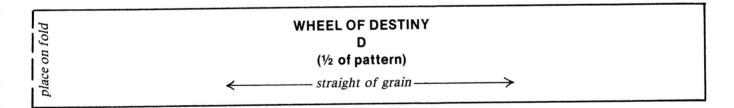

place on fold

**WHEEL OF DESTINY
D
(½ of pattern)**

←————— straight of grain —————→

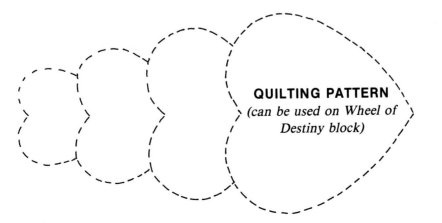

QUILTING PATTERN
*(can be used on Wheel of
Destiny block)*

3

Tote bags

Tote bags ought to be sturdy, able to transport a multitude of things. That's why the basic fabric for each of our sample bags is heavier than the design fabric stitched to it.

We chose fabrics woven for slipcovers, jeans and other sportswear. When a pieced work design was framed with sashing, we used the heavier tote fabric for the sashing (see Signs of Spring tote, page 121).

There are six pattern choices in this chapter, but if you'd rather have one of the pillow designs from Chapter 2 on your tote bag, go ahead and use it. The finished blocks are all the same size.

You also could borrow one of the crib quilt appliqués from Chapter 6. Just sew it on a tote-size block. It will look fine.

Pieced designs are best quilted, and this can be done by hand or by machine. Appliqués can be quilted or not (we skipped it in most cases); but if the fabric is sturdy, you'll probably have to quilt by machine.

To help the bags hold their shapes, we added a firm, non-fusible interfacing to most. It's cut the same size as the main tote sections, then the tote fabric and interfacing are handled as one for stitching.

Most of the bags are lined, too. A bag that's quilted or interfaced should be lined. But one made of sturdy fabric without quilting or interfacing, such as our denim bag with the Peeping Cat on page 30, works without a lining.

Handle length can be varied. You can make handles for a shoulder bag or cut shorter ones for hand carrying.

Look under the heading for each pattern to find a list of materials and special instructions. Then use the general directions that follow.

To make a tote bag

1. Complete tote bag front, following directions for the pattern you choose. If block is to be quilted or interfaced, machine-stitch on the seam (pencil) line around edge.

2. Quilt if desired. (This is optional for appliqué.)

To quilt, mark any needed guidelines. Then stack layers in this order: muslin (or other backing fabric); batting; tote front, right side up. Baste together and quilt. (See *General guides for quilting*, page 5.)

Finally, baste layers together around the edge, sewing directly over the seam line.

3. Cut tote pieces (Fig. 1). On *wrong* side of fabric, mark one 15″ square for back; three 4x15″ pieces, for sides and bottom; one 4x35″ piece for facing; and two 4x21″ pieces, for shoulder handles (or 4x15″ for shorter handles). Cut fabric on marked lines; ½″ seam allowances are included.

Note: For 32″-wide striped ticking, cut front and back pieces across top of fabric. Cut sides, bottom, handles and facing below, with the longest edges of all pieces placed vertically, running along the stripes. Facing must be cut in two 4x18″ pieces.

4. Cut interfacing (optional). Cut two 15″ squares, for front and back, and three 4x15″ pieces, for sides and bottom. Pin interfacing to wrong side of tote sections and baste layers together.

5. Stitch tote. On wrong side of bottom piece, mark ½″ seam allowances with pencil. To make boxing, see Fig. 2. Join each

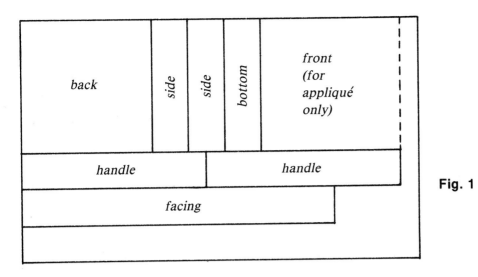

back	side	side	bottom	front (for appliqué only)
handle			handle	
facing				

Fig. 1   *Layout for tote bag, using 44"-wide fabric*

side to the bottom, stitching only on seam (pencil) lines; do not stitch into seam allowances. Press seams open.

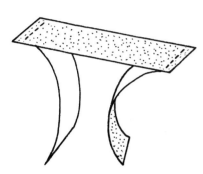

Fig. 2   *Stitching boxing*

Pin boxing to front, right sides together; match seam lines at corners. (If the front is pieced work, basting along the seam lines first will give you guidelines to help keep pattern exact.) Machine-stitch ½" seams, with boxing on top; pivot at each corner.

Pin and stitch boxing to back in same manner.

Do not press seams open; press side seams toward front and back, away from boxing.

Turn tote right side out. Fold fabric on boxing seams and press to square-up bag.

Note: If tote will not be lined, finish each seam as it is stitched.

Overcast raw edges with a zig-zag stitch, or use a straight stitch close to the raw edge.

6. Add handles. Fold each handle in half lengthwise, right side out, and press. Open fabric and fold each raw edge to center on wrong side; press. Refold lengthwise and press. Topstitch close to each edge.

On tote front, find the center along top edge. Measure 3" to each side of center and mark; center ends of one handle on each mark (Fig. 3). Keep raw edges of handle even with raw edge of tote. Machine-stitch across handle several times. Add handle to back in same manner.

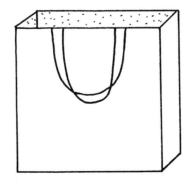

Fig. 3   *Adding handles*

7. Add facing to top. Stitch short ends of facing, right sides together, to form a ring; press seam open.

Pin facing to top of tote, right sides together. Machine-stitch ½" from raw edges (Fig. 4), following seam line on tote front.

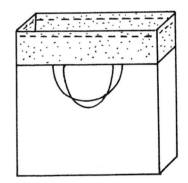

Fig. 4   *Adding facing*

Press facing and seam allowances away from tote. Topstitch facing close to seam line, through seam allowances (Fig. 5). (This will help keep facing out of sight.)

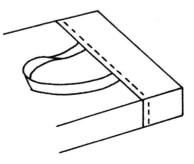

Fig. 5   *Topstitching facing*

Turn raw edge of facing ½"
to wrong side, press and stitch.
Press facing to inside of tote.

If bag will not be lined, hem
facing to bag by hand.

8. Cut and add lining (optional). From lining fabric, mark
and cut two 12x15" pieces, for
front and back; two 4x12"
pieces, for sides; and one 4x15"
piece for bottom. Seam allowances of ½" are included.

On wrong side of bottom
piece, mark ½" seam allowances. Join sides to bottom to
form boxing, then stitch boxing
to front and back, following
Step 5, page 28.

Place lining inside tote, wrong
sides together. Match seams on
boxing, and let turned edge of
facing overlap raw edge of lining by ½". Sew facing to lining
by hand.

To keep the bottom flat, you
can add a 2¾x13¾" piece of
heavy cardboard. Leave it plain
or cover it with fabric, and
place it in bottom of tote.

BIG SUN

Fig. 6 Big Sun
(color photo, page 120)

Our orange sun is cut in one
piece. We did the appliquéing
and embroidery by machine,
using yellow-gold thread, but
you could do the work by hand.

Materials
*¾ yd. off-white fabric, 44"
wide, for bag
orange fabric, 12x12"
lightweight, fusible interfacing,
12x12" (for machine appliqué)
thread for stitching
yellow-gold embroidery floss or
thread, for embroidery lines
for quilting (optional): polyester
batting, 15x15"; muslin or
similar fabric, 15x15"; thread
for bag interfacing (optional):
⅝ yd. firm interfacing, 44"
wide
for lining (optional): ½ yd.
fabric, 44" wide*

Directions
See *General guides for appliqué*,
page 2.
1. Trace Big Sun pattern, pages
34-35, joining sections as noted.
Use the paper tracing to transfer
appliqué outline and inside design lines to right side of fabric.
2. On *wrong* side of off-white
fabric, mark a 14" square for
front of bag. Cut out, adding a

½" seam allowance.
3. Use orange fabric to prepare
and cut appliqué (in one piece)
for either hand or machine
stitching.
4. Center sun on right side of
front block and sew in place.
5. Add embroidery lines in yellow-gold.
6. Cut tote pieces and finish
bag; see *To make a tote bag,*
page 28.

PEEPING CAT

Fig. 7 Peeping Cat
(color photo, page 120)

Our sturdy denim tote bag was
constructed as simply as
possible—it has no quilting,
interfacing or lining. The cat
was appliquéd with red thread,
then embroidered in blue. Red
stitching outlines the rug.

Materials
*¾ yd. denim, 44" wide, for bag
red fabric, 9x12", for cat
navy blue and red print, 7x12",
for rug
lightweight, fusible interfacing,
12x16" (for machine appliqué)
thread for stitching
navy blue and red embroidery
floss or thread, for embroidery lines*

Directions
See *General guides for appliqué*,
page 2.

1. Trace Peeping Cat pattern, pages 36-37, joining sections as noted. Make a separate template for cat and rug.

2. On *wrong* side of denim fabric, mark a 14″ square for front block. Cut out, adding a ½″ seam allowance.

3. Prepare and cut appliqué pieces for either hand or machine stitching. Use red fabric for cat (cut in one piece) and print for rug.

4. Center appliqués on right side of front block and sew in place, using red thread for cat. For handwork, you can emphasize the rug with a blanket stitch in red floss.

5. Add embroidery lines on cat in navy blue.

6. Cut tote pieces and finish bag; see *To make a tote bag,* page 28.

BOUQUET

Fig. 8   Bouquet
       (color photo, page 120)

This appliqué is cut in one piece, then the flowers are stitched in red and the leaves are stitched in green. To create a mixed bouquet, you could cut each flower and leaf separately, using a variety of colors and fabrics.

Materials

¾ yd. red fabric, 44″ wide, for bag

white fabric, 13x13″, for design

lightweight, fusible interfacing, 13x13″ (for machine appliqué)

thread for stitching

red and green embroidery floss or thread, for embroidery lines

for quilting (optional): polyester batting, 15x15″; muslin or similar fabric, 15x15″; thread

for bag interfacing (optional): ⅝ yd. firm interfacing, 44″ wide

for lining (optional): ½ yd. fabric, 44″ wide

Directions

See *General guides for appliqué,* page 2.

1. Trace Bouquet pattern, pages 38-39, joining sections as noted. Use this to transfer appliqué outline and inside design lines to fabric.

2. On *wrong* side of red fabric, mark a 14″ square for front of bag. Cut out, adding a ½″ seam allowance.

3. Use white fabric to prepare and cut appliqué (in one piece) for either hand or machine stitching.

4. Center bouquet on right side of front block and sew in place.

5. Add embroidery lines, using red for flowers and green for leaves.

6. Cut tote pieces and finish bag; see *To make a tote bag,* page 28.

FOLDED ROSE

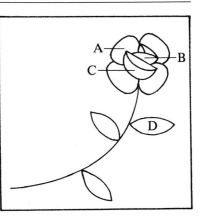

Fig. 9   Folded Rose
       (color photo, page 121)

This appliqué is three-dimensional and should be attached by hand. The two center petals are made double, then folded before being sewn in place. (If you wish to do machine appliqué, substitute the Flat Rose pattern on page 99.) Our sample bag is made of ticking, with interfacing and a lining.

Materials

1⅛ yd. striped ticking, 32″ wide, for bag

¾ yd. rose fabric, 44″ wide, for design and lining

green fabric, 5x6″, for leaves

12″ green double-fold bias binding, ¼″ wide, for stem

thread for stitching

for quilting (optional): polyester batting, 15x15″; muslin or similar fabric, 15x15″; thread

for bag interfacing (optional): ⅝ yd. firm interfacing, 44″ wide

Directions

See *General guides for appliqué,* page 2.

1. Trace pattern pieces A-D for Folded Rose, page 40. Make a template for each piece.

2. On *wrong* side of ticking,

mark a 14″ square for front block. Cut out, adding a ½″ seam allowance.

Cut off 6″ across top of rose fabric to use for appliqué pieces; save remainder for bag lining.

3. Place templates on *right* side of fabric. On rose, trace one A and one A-reversed. On green, trace three D pieces. Cut out, adding a ¼″ seam allowance.

Fold rose fabric double, *wrong* side out, and trace one B and one C. Cut out layers, adding a ¼″ seam allowance.

4. Prepare petals A for hand stitching. (You may have to underline them with white to prevent see-through.)

Machine-stitch the two B pieces, right sides together, on the seam (pencil) line; leave bottom edge open. Machine-stitch C layers together, leaving 1″ open for turning.

Press seams open, trim to ⅛″, and clip out V-shaped pieces on curves to reduce bulk. Turn to right side, work seam to edge and press.

Close seam opening on C with hand stitches; leave raw edge on B unfinished.

Fold petal B along fold lines shown on pattern (Fig. 10), and catch at bottom with basting.

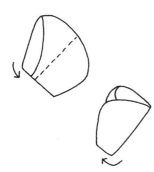

Fig. 10 *Folding inner petal B*

Fold petal C along fold line shown on pattern, and take a few stitches at each side to hold.

5. For stem, prepare double-fold bias by cutting away one fold along the length of the strip. This gives you a narrow single-fold bias—narrower than you can buy ready-made.

6. Position appliqué pieces on right side of front block. Rose should be 2″ from top seam line and 2½″ from right seam line. Layer A pieces diagonally in a cross (Fig. 11). Pin bias stem to ticking (see Fig. 9). Tuck top end of bias under petals; turn a ¼″ hem at bottom. Sew bias in place.

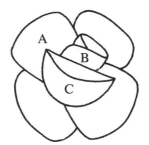

Fig. 11 *Layering A petals*

Sew petals A in place.
Position petals B and C (Fig. 12). Sew B along top, sides and

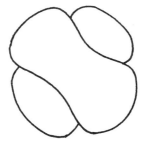

Fig. 12 *Adding top petals*

bottom (not on folded curves). Sew C along bottom curve.
7. Cut tote pieces and finish bag; see *To make a tote bag,* page 28.

WILL-O'-THE-WISP

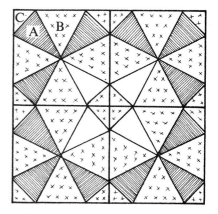

Fig. 13 Will-o'-the-Wisp *(color photo, page 121)*

The basic design is repeated four times. In each square, one A triangle is light blue, while the others are medium blue. These lighter pieces form a secondary design at the center of the finished block.

Materials

¾ yd. medium-dark blue fabric, 44″ wide, for bag
¾ yd. blue print, 44″ wide, for design and lining
medium blue fabric, 6x28″, for design
light blue fabric, 6x11″, for design
polyester batting, 15x15″, for quilting
muslin or similar fabric, 15x15″, for quilting
thread for stitching and quilting
for bag interfacing (optional):
⅝ yd. firm interfacing, 44″ wide

Directions

See *General guides for pieced work,* page 5.
1. Trace pattern pieces A-C for Will-o'-the-Wisp, page 40. Make a template for each piece.

2. Cut off 10" across top of blue print to use for pieced block; save remainder for bag lining.

3. Place templates on *wrong* side of fabric. On blue print, trace 16 B and 16 C pieces. On medium blue solid, trace 12 A pieces. On light blue, trace four A pieces. Cut out, adding a ½" seam allowance.

4. Lay pieces flat, right side up, to form design in Fig. 13. To assemble half of a small square (Fig. 14), join each A to a C, then add the B pieces.

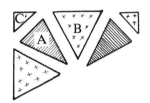

Fig. 14 *Joining half a small square*

Complete other half of square and join the two halves. Finish all squares, and join them to complete the block.

5. Quilt block, cut tote pieces and finish bag; see *To make a tote bag,* page 28.

SIGNS OF SPRING

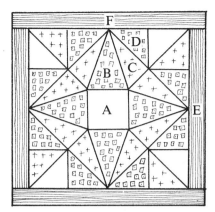

Fig. 15 Signs of Spring *(color photo, page 121)*

Bright yellow and green fabrics give this tote a true spring look. Use the bag fabric for sashing to frame the pieced design.

Materials

¾ yd. green fabric, 44" wide, for bag and sashing
¾ yd. green print, 44" wide, for design and lining
yellow print, 9x18", for design
yellow fabric, 9x10", for design
polyester batting, 15x15", for quilting
muslin or similar fabric, 15x15", for quilting
thread for stitching and quilting
for bag interfacing (optional): ⅝ yd. firm interfacing, 44" wide

Directions

See *General guides for pieced work,* page 5.

1. Trace pattern pieces A-F for Signs of Spring, page 41. Make a template for each piece.

2. Cut off 6" across top of green print to use for pieced block; save remainder for bag lining.

3. Place templates on *wrong* side of fabric. On yellow, trace one A and four D pieces. On green print, trace four B and eight D pieces. On yellow print, trace four C, four C-reversed and four D pieces. On green fabric, trace two E and two F pieces. Cut out, adding a ½" seam allowance.

4. Lay pieces flat, right side up, to form design in Fig. 15.

Complete each corner by joining a yellow D to a yellow print D (Fig. 16). Then add two green print D pieces to make a large triangle.

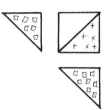

Fig. 16 *Forming corners*

Join a B to each side of center A (Fig. 17), stitching only on seam (pencil) lines; do not stitch into seam allowances. Join each pair of C pieces. Then add C units to center section, pivoting at corners of A.

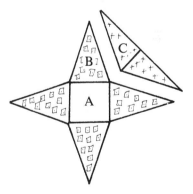

Fig. 17 *Piecing center of block*

Add corner triangles to form a square. Stitch an E to each side, then an F to top and bottom to complete the block.

5. Quilt block, cut tote pieces and finish bag; see *To make a tote bag,* page 28.

short broken lines
are embroidery lines

join to right side on broken line

BIG SUN
(left side)

join to left side on broken line

short broken lines
are embroidery lines

BIG SUN
(right side)

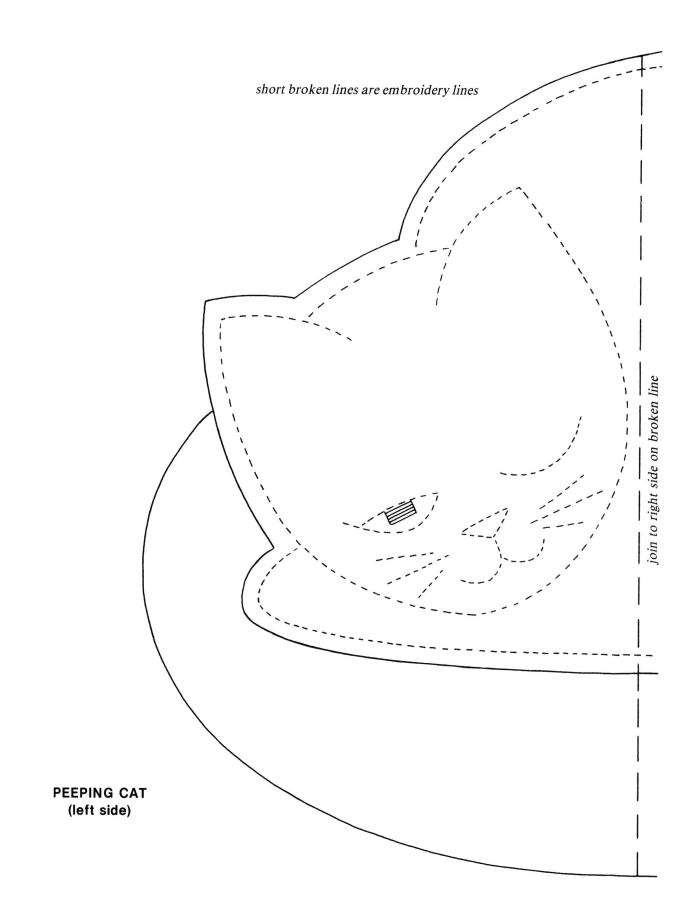

short broken lines are embroidery lines

join to right side on broken line

PEEPING CAT
(left side)

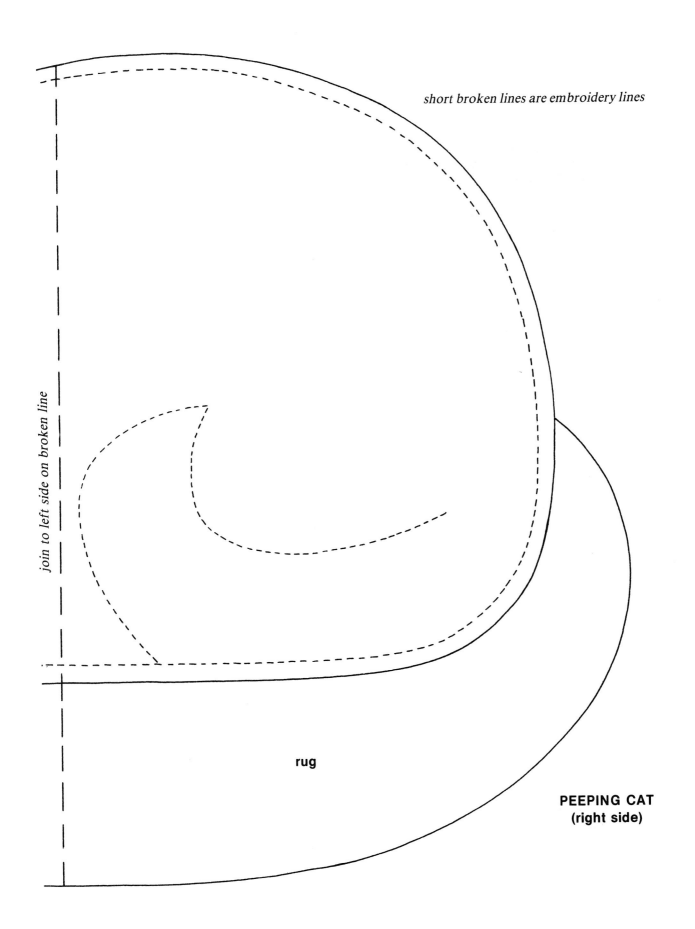

short broken lines are embroidery lines

join to left side on broken line

rug

PEEPING CAT
(right side)

short broken lines are embroidery lines

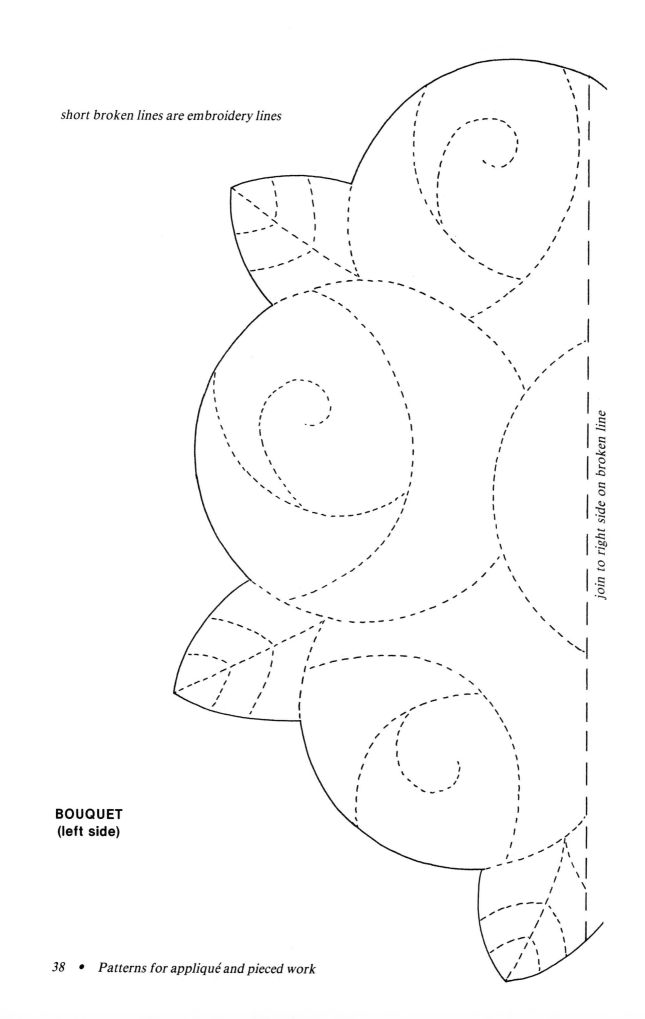

join to right side on broken line

**BOUQUET
(left side)**

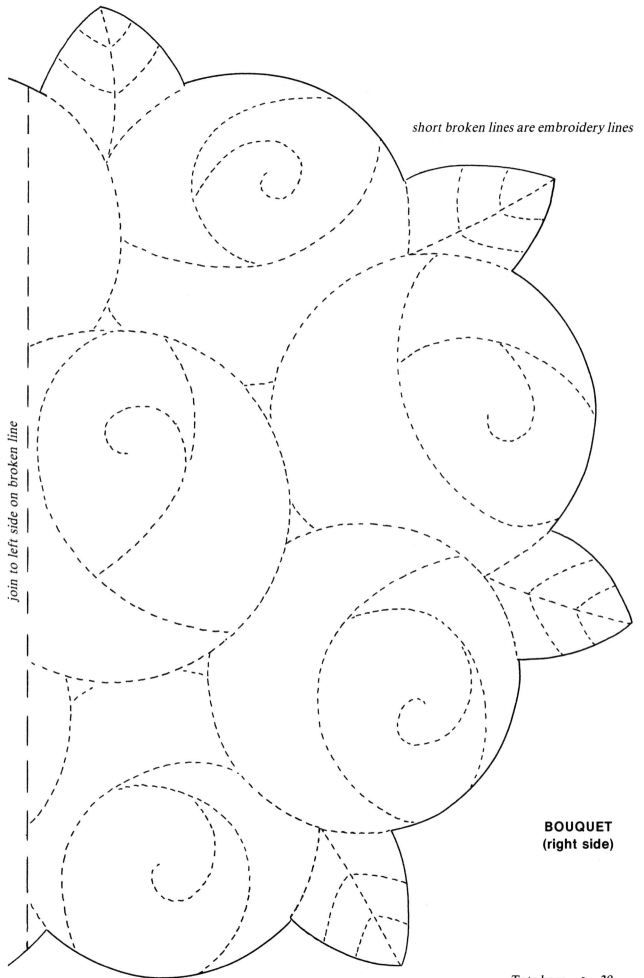

short broken lines are embroidery lines

join to left side on broken line

BOUQUET
(right side)

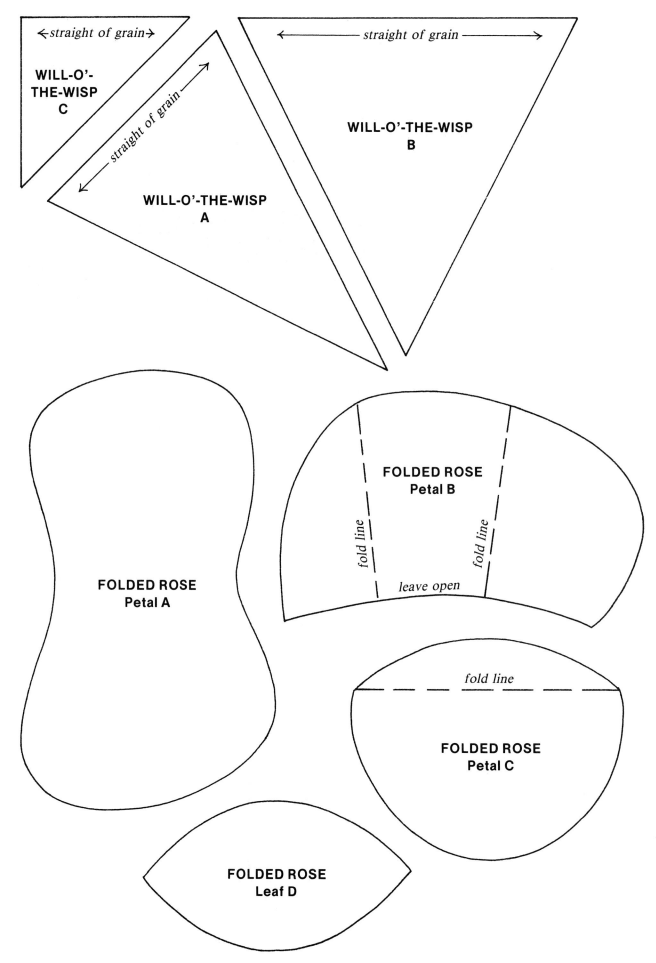

←*straight of grain*→

WILL-O'-THE-WISP C

straight of grain

WILL-O'-THE-WISP A

←———— *straight of grain* ————→

WILL-O'-THE-WISP B

FOLDED ROSE Petal A

FOLDED ROSE Petal B

fold line

fold line

leave open

fold line

FOLDED ROSE Petal C

FOLDED ROSE Leaf D

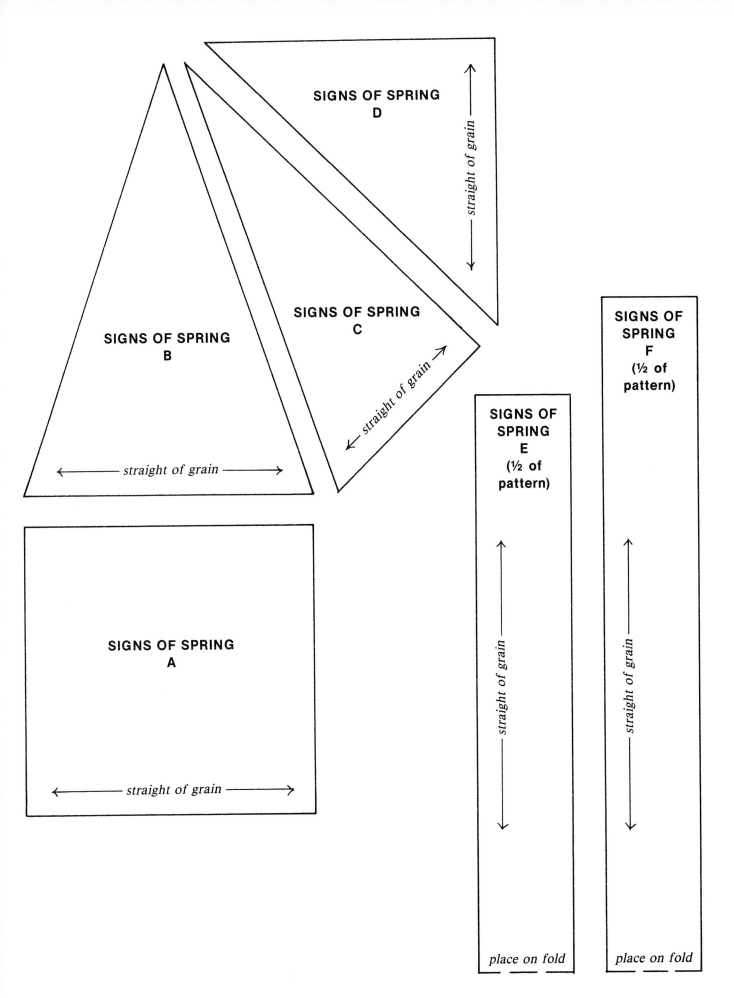

SIGNS OF SPRING
D

straight of grain

SIGNS OF SPRING
B

SIGNS OF SPRING
C

SIGNS OF SPRING
F
(½ of
pattern)

straight of grain

SIGNS OF SPRING
E
(½ of
pattern)

straight of grain

straight of grain

SIGNS OF SPRING
A

straight of grain

straight of grain

straight of grain

place on fold

place on fold

4
Placemats

One way to create a light mealtime mood is to set a pretty table, and these placemats (three appliquéd and four pieced) are designed to do just that.

For a splashy look with the least amount of work, try the Rainbow, page 44; it has just six design pieces. The only challenge is to make all the points meet at the center.

For a country look, consider the Sunny Morning appliqué with its sun face quilted in green, or the blue and white pieced work pattern called Pleasant Paths.

You'll want to make a set of most placemats—at least two. However, the Happy Clown can be a "single" made for one special youngster.

To make a matching napkin for any design, just cut an 18" square of fabric, make two ¼" turns for the hem, and stitch.

Be sure to choose colorfast fabrics, and preshrink them before cutting (see page 1). Choose a thin batting to keep the placemat rather flat (and the dishes level).

Look under the heading for each design to find a list of materials needed and any special instructions. Then follow the general directions below to make the placemat.

Do take a second look at these placemat designs and picture them as pillows. Quilt the block before you stitch it to the back (see page 7). You can make a separate inner pillow or just attach the front to a back and stuff.

To make a placemat

1. Complete placemat front, following directions for individual pattern. Mark any needed quilting lines.

2. Stitch front to back. Cut batting to fit back. Then stack layers in this order: batting; back, right side up; front, right side down. Pin edges and stitch over seam line on front; leave 6" open for turning.

Trim batting close to stitching. Trim seams to ¼" and clip across any corners. Turn placemat to right side and close opening with hand stitches. Work seam to edge, baste, and press lightly.

3. Quilt. Baste layers together and quilt as desired; see *General guides for quilting,* page 5.

RED APPLE

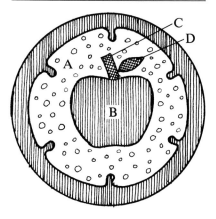

Fig. 1   Red Apple
(color photo, page 49)

Now you can have two apples a day—one on your placemat.

Materials
½ yd. red fabric, 44" wide, for front, back and apple
white print, 16x16", for A
polyester batting, 18x18"
green scrap, for leaf and stem
½ yd. lightweight, fusible interfacing, 22" wide (for machine appliqué)
thread for stitching and quilting

Directions
See *General guides for appliqué,* page 2.
1. Fold a 16" square of tracing paper in half, then fold again to

divide into quarters. Open paper and position over Red Apple pattern, page 52, with folds of paper on top of broken lines. The center fold of paper should be over center point of design (noted on pattern). Trace curves for A, and copy apple placement lines.

To complete pattern, refold tracing paper in half vertically. With traced section on the bottom, copy lines for A onto top layer (do not copy apple). Refold tracing paper in half horizontally. With traced half on bottom, copy lines for A onto top layer.

Open tracing paper and position over apple pattern, page 53. Trace rest of apple. Make a template for each piece, A-D.

2. To make a pattern for placemat front and back, draw a 17" circle (8½" radius) on tracing or other paper, and cut out.

3. Fold red fabric in half, wrong side out. Trace 17" circle pattern on top layer (leave enough fabric at fold to cut one B on single layer later). Cut out both layers, adding a ½" seam allowance to circle.

On top layer (front), machine-stitch directly over seam (pencil) line.

4. Prepare and cut appliqué pieces for either hand or machine stitching. Use white print for one A. Use red for one B, and green for one C and one D.

5. Center appliqué pieces on right side of front circle (see Fig. 1); place A first, then apple pieces. Sew in place.

6. Stitch front to back and quilt; see *To make a placemat*, page 42.

SUNNY DAY

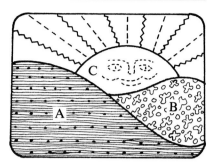

Fig. 2 Sunny Day
(color photo, page 48)

Rolling green hills and a smiling sun can brighten any breakfast table. Quilt the face in green if you want it to show up well.

Materials
½ yd. green fabric with white dots, 44" wide, for Hill A and back
white fabric, 15x20", for front
green flower print, 7x11", for Hill B
yellow fabric, 6x10", for Sun face
½ yd. lightweight, fusible interfacing, 22" wide (for machine appliqué)
1 yd. yellow baby rickrack, for sunrays
polyester batting, 14x19"
thread for stitching and quilting

Directions
See *General guides for appliqué*, page 2.

1. On a 15x20" sheet of tracing paper, trace Sunny Day pattern, pages 54-57, joining the four sections as noted. Copy all inside design lines, and make one template for Hill A, one for Hill B and one for Sun face C.

2. Cut out large Sunny Day tracing paper pattern on outside lines. Place the pattern on *wrong* side of white fabric, and trace the outline. Cut out fabric, adding a ½" seam allowance.

Machine-stitch around the edge, directly over seam (pencil) line. This is the background fabric for front of placemat.

For the back, place tracing paper pattern on *wrong* side of green dotted fabric and trace outline. Cut out fabric, adding a ½" seam allowance.

3. Prepare and cut appliqué pieces for either hand or machine stitching. No matter which method you use, add a ½" seam allowance to the left side and bottom of Hill A and to the right side of Hill B. These will extend into the placemat seam allowance and be caught in the seam.

Use green dotted fabric for one Hill A, green flower print for one Hill B, and yellow fabric for one Sun face C. Hill B overlaps Sun face; Hill A overlaps Sun face and Hill B.

4. Position rickrack and appliqué pieces on right side of placemat front. One end of each rickrack strip is overlapped ¼" by the Sun face; other end extends into placemat seam allowance. Sew rickrack and appliqués in place.

5. Stitch front to back and quilt; see *To make a placemat*, page 42. Quilt face in green, and quilt lines between rickrack in white. To quilt the hills, follow shapes of the appliqués.

CLOWN FACE

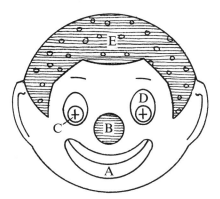

Fig. 3   Clown Face
            (color photo, page 49)

This happy clown should make
any youngster smile whenever
the two meet at mealtime.

Materials

*½ yd. yellow fabric, 44″ wide,
   for front and back
white fabric, 9x9″, for eyes and
   mouth
bright blue scrap, for inner eyes
red scrap, for nose
red print (with yellow), 12x17″,
   for hair
½ yd. lightweight, fusible interfacing, 22″ wide (for machine
   appliqué)
polyester batting, 18x20″
thread for stitching and quilting
black embroidery floss or
   thread, for embroidery lines*

Directions

See *General guides for appliqué,*
page 2.
1. Fold a 20″ square of tracing
paper in half, then fold again to
divide into quarters. Open paper
and position over Clown Face
pattern, pages 58-59, with folds
of paper on top of broken lines.
The center fold of paper should
be over center point of placemat
(noted on pattern). Trace upper
right and lower right sections,
joining the two sections as
noted.

To complete pattern, refold
tracing paper in half. With
traced side on bottom, copy pattern onto left side. Make templates for pattern pieces A-E.
2. Cut out large Clown Face
tracing paper pattern on outside
lines. Fold yellow fabric in half,
wrong side out. Place Clown
Face pattern on top layer and
trace around the outside. Cut
out both layers of fabric, adding
a ½″ seam allowance. On top
layer (front), machine-stitch
around edge directly over seam
(pencil) line.
3. Prepare and cut appliqué
pieces for either hand or machine stitching. No matter which
method you choose, add a ½″
seam allowance to the top curve
of E (hair). This will extend into
the placemat seam allowance
and be caught in the seam.
   Use white for one A (mouth)
and two D (outer eye) pieces,
blue for two C (inner eye)
pieces, red for one B (nose), and
red print for one E (hair) piece.
4. Position appliqué pieces on
right side of yellow front and
sew in place. (For machine
work, stitch eyes and mouth
with black thread.)
5. Add embroidery lines. Use
black for center line on mouth,
center cross in eyes, and lines
for eyebrows and ears. If appliqué was done by hand with
matching thread, use black floss
to embroider around eyes and
mouth.
6. Stitch front to back and
quilt. See *To make a placemat,*
page 42.

RAINBOW

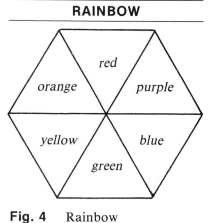

Fig. 4   Rainbow
            (color photo, page 48)

You can produce this spectacular look with only one basic
pattern and a few quilting lines.
Youngsters love the bright colors, and they'll have fun learn-
ing the color wheel.

Materials

*6 fabrics (red, orange, yellow,
   green, blue, purple), 10x11″
   each
print fabric, 18x20″, for back
polyester batting, 18x20″
thread for stitching and quilting*

Directions

See *General guides for pieced
work,* page 5.
1. Trace pattern for Rainbow
Triangle, page 60, and make a
template.
   To draw back pattern, use a
large sheet of tracing paper and
trace the same Rainbow
Triangle six times, butting sides
together to complete a hexagon
(Fig. 4). Cut out pattern on outside lines.
2. Place template and back pattern on *wrong* side of fabric. On
each color, trace one triangle.
On print, trace one hexagon
back. Cut out fabric, adding a
½″ seam allowance.
3. Lay triangles flat, right side
up, to form design in Fig. 4.
4. Pin two triangles, right sides

together. Begin stitching at outside raw edge, and stop exactly on the seam line at center of design; do not stitch into the seam allowance. Add one more triangle in the same manner to complete half the design. Press all seam allowances flat and in the same direction; trim to ⅛".

Repeat to complete other half of design.

Join the two halves, making sure that all points meet at center. (You may want to baste the center area before stitching.) Press seam, and trim to ⅛".
5. Stitch front to back and quilt; see *To make a placemat*, page 42.

HEXAGON BEAUTY

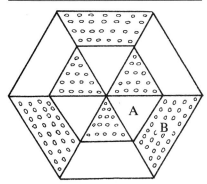

Fig. 5　Hexagon Beauty
(*color photo, page 48*)

A print fabric alternates with a plain color to form this traditional design.

Materials
½ yd. blue fabric, 44" wide, for design and back
¼ yd. blue and yellow print, 44" wide, for design
polyester batting, 18x20"
thread for stitching and quilting

Directions
See *General guides for pieced work,* page 5.
1. Trace pattern pieces A and B

for Hexagon Beauty, page 60. Make a template for each piece.

To draw a hexagon back pattern, follow Step 1 of Rainbow Placemat at left.
2. Place back pattern and templates on *wrong* side of fabric. On blue, trace one back, three A and three B pieces. On print, trace three A and three B pieces. Cut out, adding a ½" seam allowance.
3. Lay pieces flat, right side up, to form design in Fig. 5. Pin each A to a B and stitch from raw edge to raw edge to form triangles. Then join triangles, following Step 4 of Rainbow Placemat at left.
4. Stitch front to back and quilt; see *To make a placemat,* page 42.

STAR FLOWER

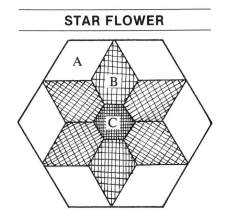

Fig. 6　Star Flower
(*color photo, page 48*)

We used brown plaid for our "flower," but you might prefer yellow to make it a daffodil.

Materials
½ yd. brown fabric, 44" wide, for design and back
¼ yd. brown plaid or stripe, 44" wide, for design
orange fabric, 6x6", for center
polyester batting, 18x20"
thread for stitching and quilting

Directions
See *General guides for pieced work,* page 5.
1. Trace pattern pieces A-C for Star Flower, page 61. Make a template for each piece.

To draw hexagon back pattern, follow Step 1 of Rainbow Placemat, page 44.
2. Place back pattern and templates A and B on *wrong* side of fabric. On brown, trace one back and six A pieces. On plaid or stripe, trace six B pieces. On the *right* side of orange fabric, trace one C. Cut out, adding a ½" seam allowance.
3. Lay pieces flat, right side up, to form design in Fig. 6. Join two B pieces, stitching only on the seam (pencil) line; do not stitch into seam allowances. Add one more B to complete

half the flower design. Press all seams flat and in the same direction, and trim to 1/8".

Repeat to complete other half of flower, and join the two halves.

Add A pieces, stitching one side at a time. With A on the bottom, stitch from raw edge to end of seam (pencil) line; do not stitch into seam allowance. Rearrange top fabric (B pieces), and stitch from end of seam line to outside raw edge.

To add orange center, turn raw edges of plaid or stripe to wrong side and press. Position orange center under opening and sew in place by hand.

4. Stitch front to back and quilt; see *To make a placemat*, page 42.

PLEASANT PATHS

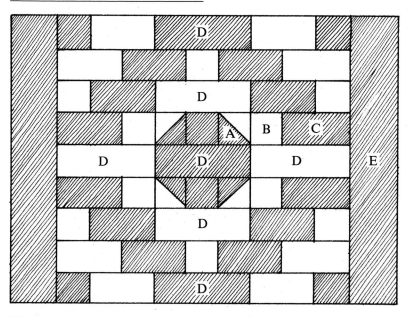

Fig. 7   Pleasant Paths
(color photo, page 49)

This pieced work design uses the original Pleasant Paths pattern, which is a rectangle. The top and bottom rows and the two side strips are new additions. Omit the side strips and you have a square—just right for a pillow top.

Materials
1/2 yd. blue print, 44" wide, for design and back
white fabric, 9x22", for design
polyester batting, 15x20"
thread for stitching and quilting

Directions
See *General guides for pieced work*, page 5.
1. Trace pattern pieces A-E for Pleasant Paths, page 51. Make a template for each piece.
2. On *wrong* side of blue print, mark a 14½x18½" rectangle for back. Cut out; ½" seam allowance is included.

Place templates on *wrong* side of fabric. On blue print, trace four A, six B, 12 C, three D and two E pieces. On white fabric, trace four A, 10 B, eight C and four D pieces. Cut out, adding a ½" seam allowance.
3. Lay pieces flat, right side up, to form design in Fig. 7. (All D pieces in diagram are labeled to help you arrange design. Other shapes are identified only once.)

Join pieces to form horizontal rows. Then join the rows, making sure seam lines meet correctly. Finally, add an E to each side to complete the block.
4. Stitch front to back and quilt; see *To make a placemat*, page 42.

Use appliqués on clothing and home furnishings that you make or buy.

Frog, page 97

Parrot, page 98

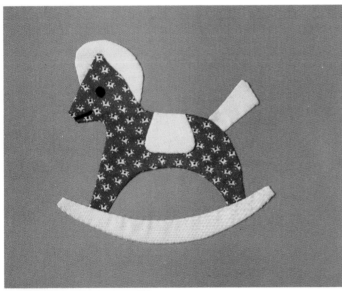

Hobby Horse, page 97

Ice Cream Cone, page 98

Lamb, page 98

Lollipop Flower, page 98

Light Bulb, page 98

48

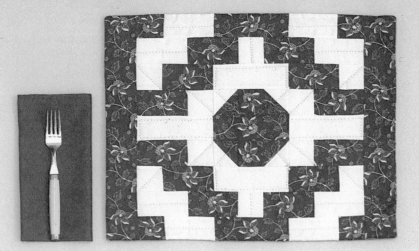

Placemats for perking up meals can be appliquéd or pieced, and Chapter 4 tells you how to make the ones shown here. On the opposite page, top to bottom, are Hexagon Beauty (page 45), Rainbow (page 44), Star Flower (page 45) and Sunny Day (page 43). On this page, top to bottom, are Pleasant Paths (page 46), Red Apple (page 42) and Clown Face (page 44).

Umbrella Girl, page 99

Sew an appliqué on something to wear, or frame one to hang on the wall.

Turtle, page 99

Penguin, page 98

Polar Bear, page 98

Snail, page 99

Little Sun, page 99

Snake, page 99

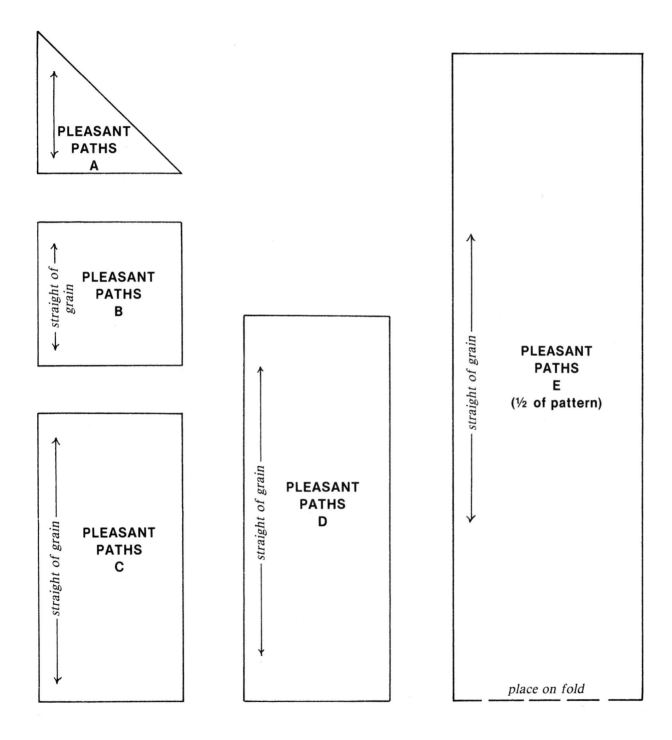

PLEASANT PATHS
A

straight of grain

PLEASANT
PATHS
B

straight of grain

PLEASANT
PATHS
C

straight of grain

PLEASANT
PATHS
D

straight of grain

PLEASANT
PATHS
E
(½ of pattern)

place on fold

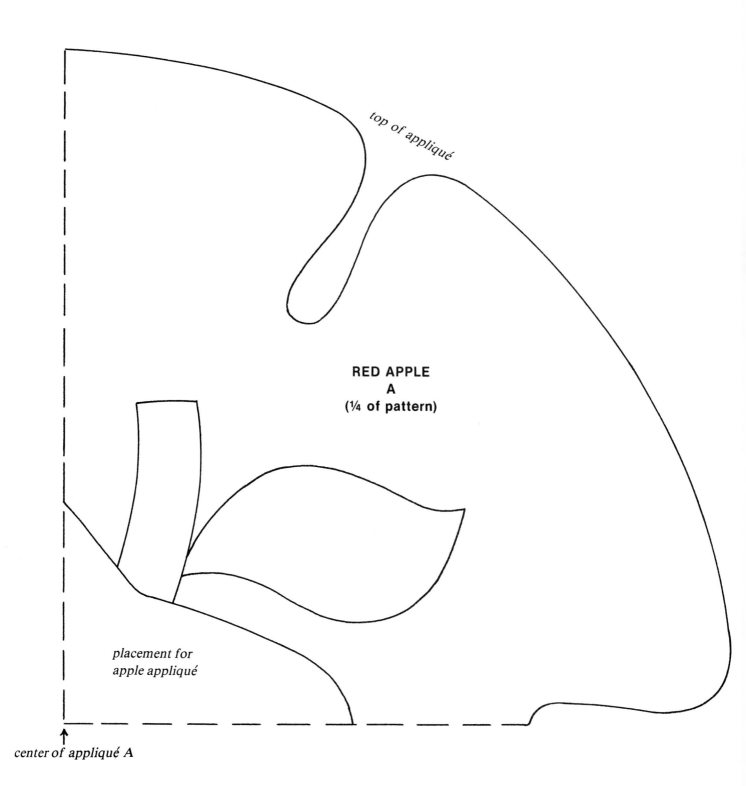

top of appliqué

RED APPLE
A
(¼ of pattern)

placement for
apple appliqué

center of appliqué A

RED APPLE
B

SUNNY DAY
(upper left section)

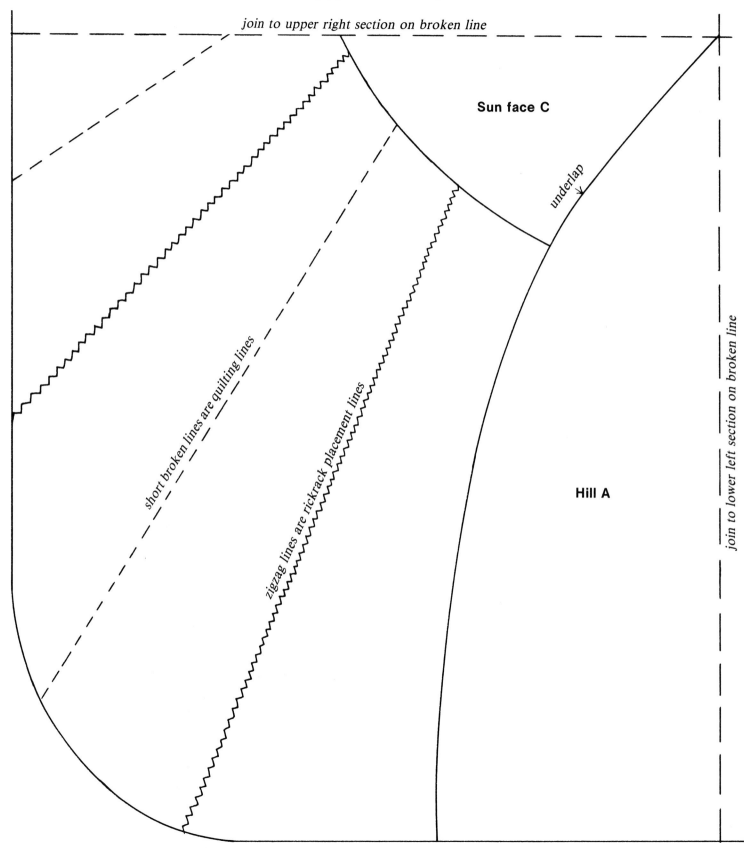

join to upper right section on broken line

Sun face C

underlap

short broken lines are quilting lines

zigzag lines are rickrack placement lines

join to lower left section on broken line

Hill A

SUNNY DAY
(lower left section)

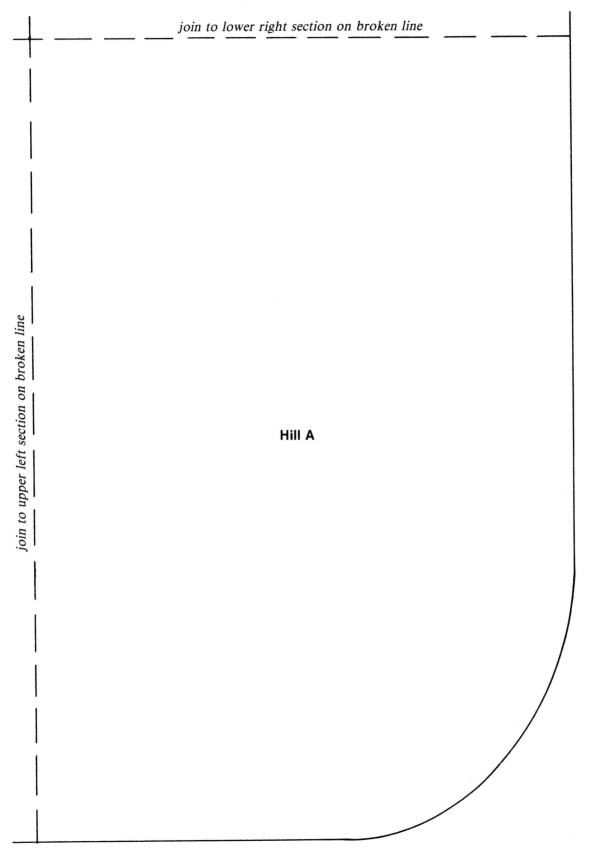

join to lower right section on broken line

join to upper left section on broken line

Hill A

SUNNY DAY
(upper right section)

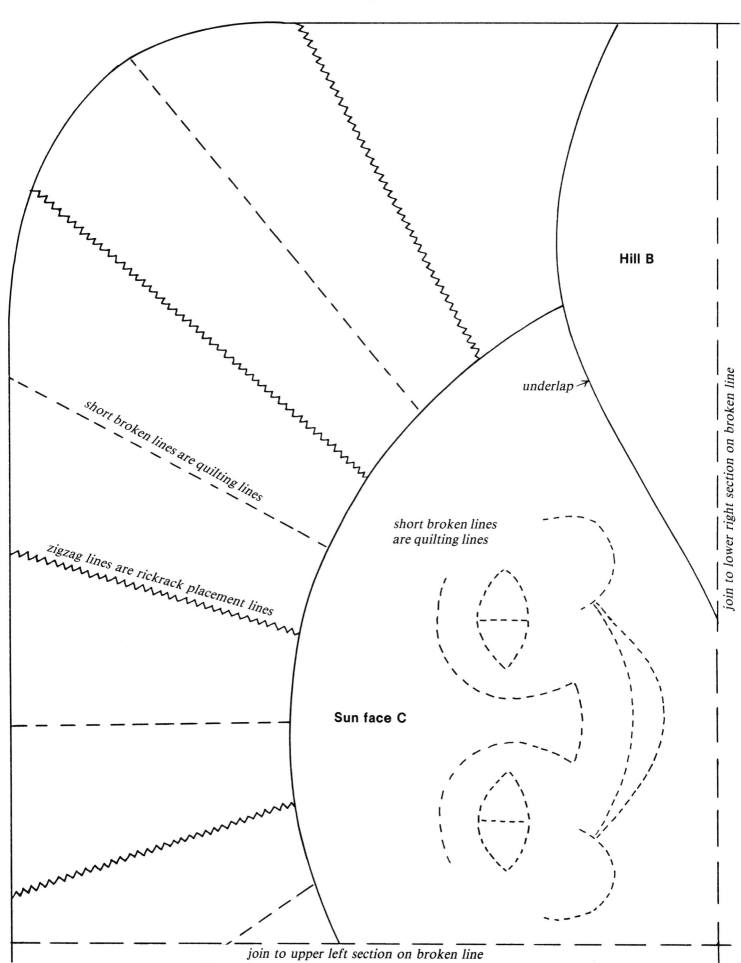

Hill B

underlap →

short broken lines are quilting lines

short broken lines
are quilting lines

zigzag lines are rickrack placement lines

Sun face C

join to lower right section on broken line

join to upper left section on broken line

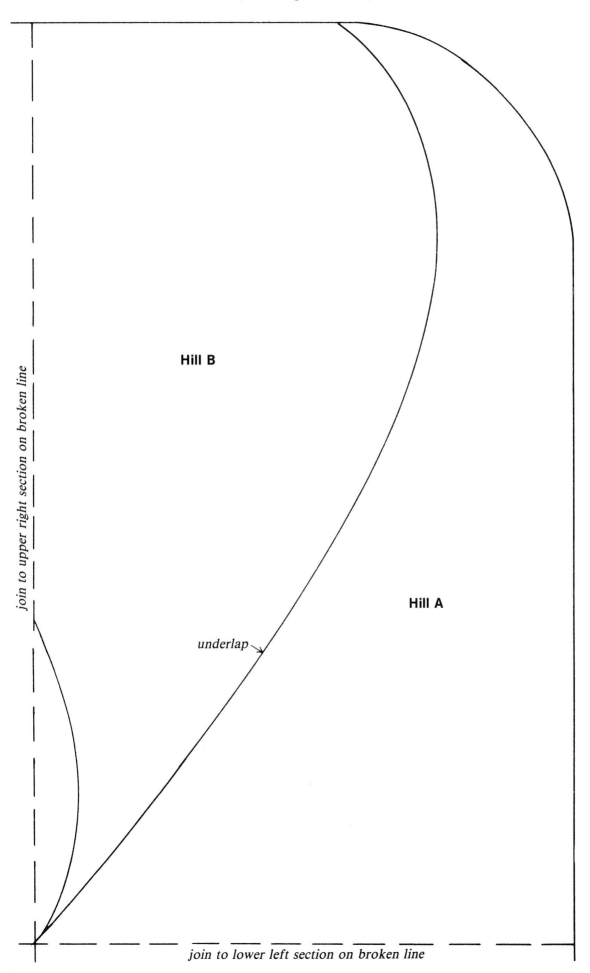

SUNNY DAY
(lower right section)

join to upper right section on broken line

Hill B

Hill A

underlap

join to lower left section on broken line

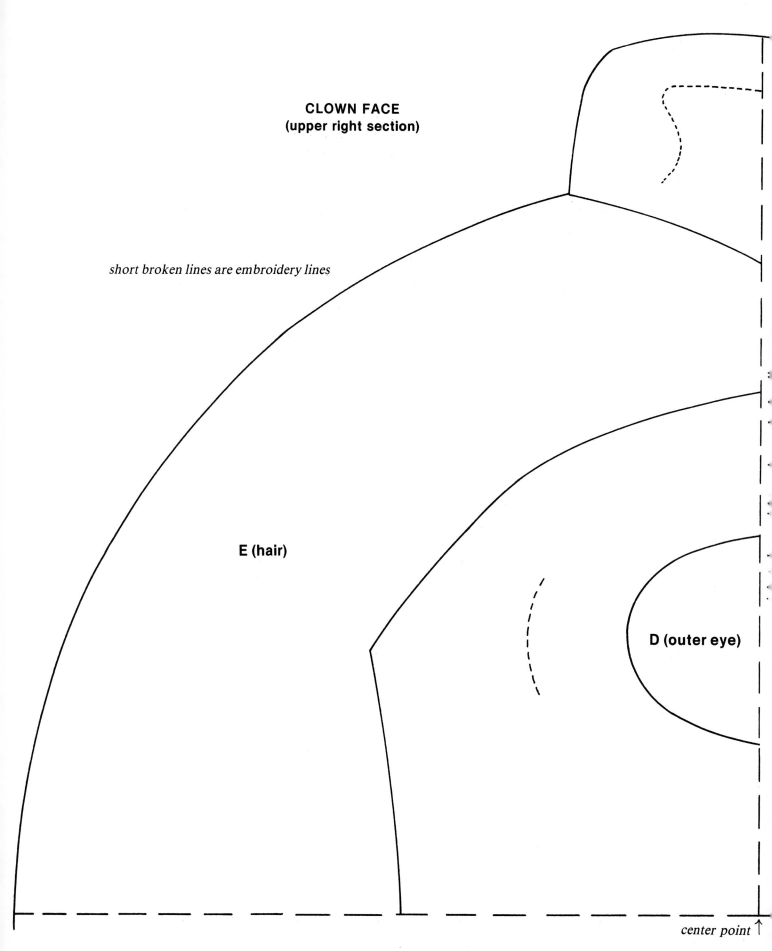

CLOWN FACE
(upper right section)

short broken lines are embroidery lines

E (hair)

D (outer eye)

center point ↑

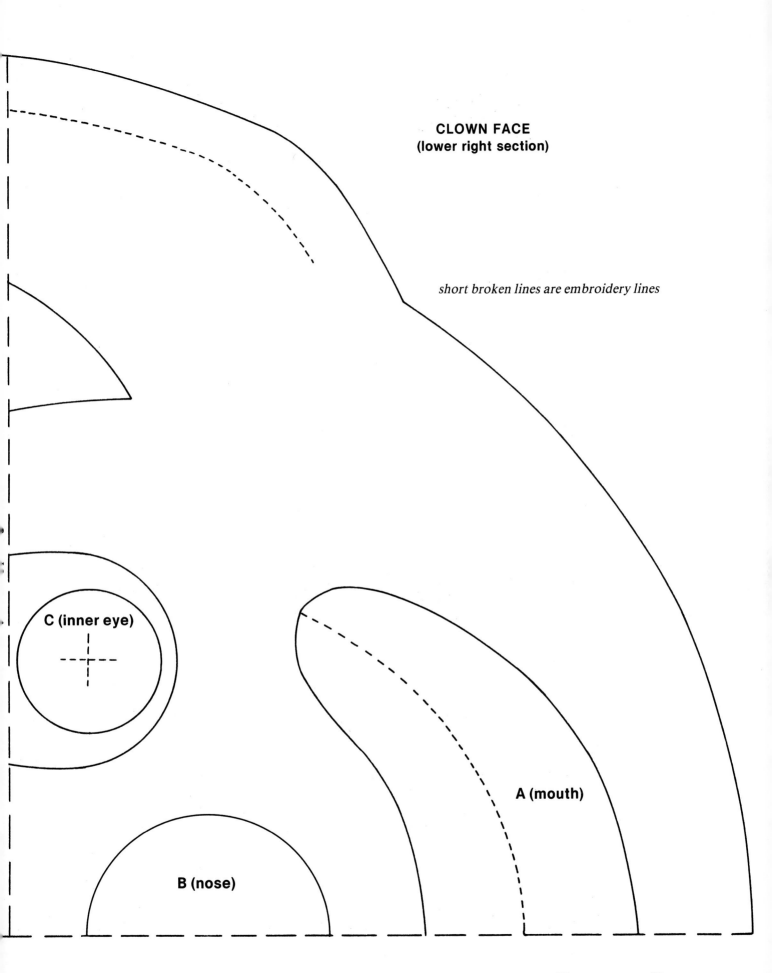

CLOWN FACE
(lower right section)

short broken lines are embroidery lines

C (inner eye)

A (mouth)

B (nose)

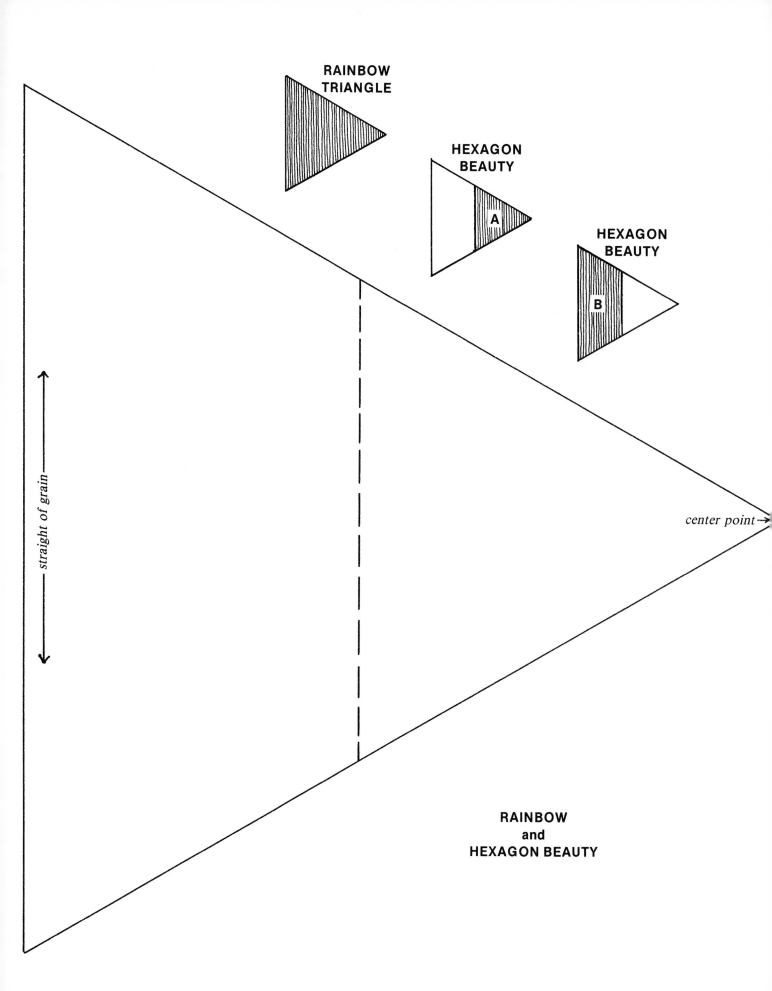

RAINBOW
TRIANGLE

HEXAGON
BEAUTY

A

HEXAGON
BEAUTY

B

straight of grain

center point →

RAINBOW
and
HEXAGON BEAUTY

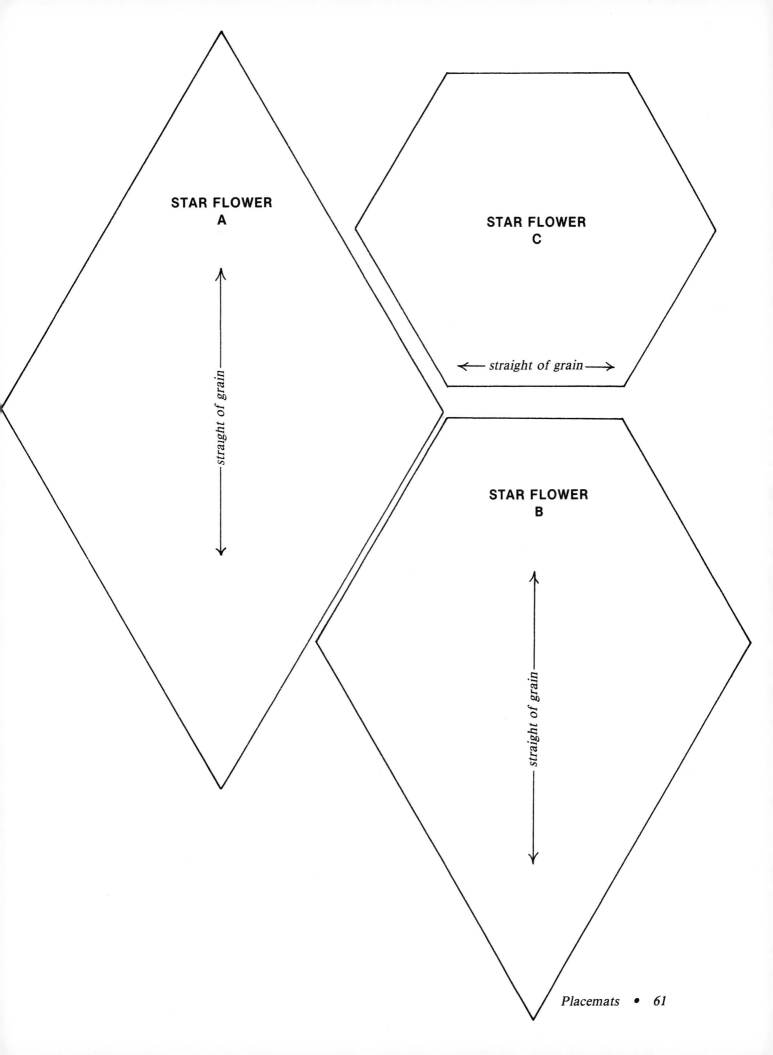

**STAR FLOWER
A**

← straight of grain →

**STAR FLOWER
C**

← straight of grain →

**STAR FLOWER
B**

← straight of grain →

5
Potholders

The ideal potholder is small enough to fit comfortably in your hand. Its padding is thick enough to protect you from the heat, yet not so bulky that the potholder tends to flop out of your hand. And, of course, it looks good.

These nine potholders pass our "user" tests. There are five appliqué and four pieced work patterns. You can do the appliqué by hand or by machine, but you'll have to quilt by machine—there are too many layers to quilt by hand.

For a quick and easy project, simply outline one of the patterns, such as our Blue Cat sample, shown on page 11. There are *General guides for outlining designs* on page 5.

Since a "working" potholder does get washed, it's especially important to preshrink fabrics and test them for colorfastness (see page 1). Why waste time and effort to make a fancy potholder, only to have it flunk its first washing?

You'll find a list of materials and special instructions under the heading for each pattern. After completing the appliqué or pieced work, follow the general directions, *To make a potholder*, given below.

Any of these appliqués could be used for other items—they aren't limited to potholders. Picture the little pig appliquéd to the center of a pillow top (substitute it for the owl on page 9). And the Question Mark would be a fun way to "fancy up" a plain shirt.

To make a potholder

1. Complete potholder front, following directions for the pattern you choose.

2. Prepare padding. Stack three layers of terry cloth; press to flatten.

Place template for back on top, and trace. Cut out fabric, adding a ¼" seam allowance. (You may want to change the number of layers, according to the thickness of the terry cloth you use. Be sure all layers of potholder will fit under machine presser foot.)

3. Quilt potholder. Stack layers in this order: back, right side down; terry cloth; front, right side up. Hand-baste together, from center to outside, and around the outside edge, just inside the seam line.

By machine, stitch (quilt) layers together. For appliqué patterns, stitch around the design, using thread to match the background.

If you like, stitch along some inside design lines, but avoid excess stitching. Otherwise, the potholder becomes compressed and too firm for easy handling.

For pieced work, use thread to blend with fabric and stitch directly over seam lines. (For Rainbow and Shadow Box, see special instructions.)

4. Prepare edge of potholder for binding. Straight-stitch by machine around the outside, directly over seam line. Fold front and back fabrics out of the way, and trim terry cloth layers close to stitching line.

Smooth front and back flat, and stitch around potholder again. This time use a zigzag stitch just outside the seam line (or use a straight stitch, ⅛" from the first stitching); keep all stitching in the seam allowance. Trim raw edges to less than ¼".

5. Add bias binding. Mark off 3½" for a loop. Position mark at top of potholder, leaving the 3½" extension free. Use matching thread to sew bias fold to stitched seam line on potholder, right sides together (Fig. 1).

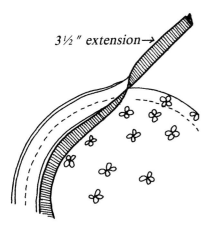

Fig. 1 *Stitching bias fold to potholder*

Take small running stitches (it is not necessary to go through all layers of fabric). Stop sewing 2" before reaching top of potholder where stitching began.

Note: For a hexagon or square potholder, take a small tuck in the bias at each corner; this adds fullness so bias will fit over edge of potholder.

To form the loop, first fold stitched bias over raw edge of potholder for several inches. Sew folded edges of the 3½" extension together. Curve this extension into a loop (Fig. 2), with ½" of the free end along the potholder edge.

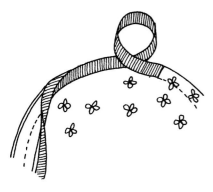

Fig. 2 *Forming bias loop*

Finish sewing bias fold to the remaining 2" of potholder, covering end of loop as you go. Cut off extra bias, leaving ¼" to turn under.

Fold bias over raw edge of potholder. By hand, sew bias to stitching on back. At the end, turn under raw edge of bias (end of loop should be completely enclosed).

BLUE CAT

Fig. 3 Blue Cat *(color photo, page 11)*

Cut the cat in one piece, and stitch the design lines in white.

Materials

2 squares white print fabric, 8x8" each, for front and back
blue fabric with white dots, 7x7", for cat
lightweight, fusible interfacing, 7x7" (for machine appliqué)
3 squares terry cloth, 8x8" each, for padding
28" blue double-fold bias binding, ¼" wide
thread for stitching and quilting
white embroidery floss or thread, for embroidery lines

Directions

See *General guides for appliqué,* page 2.
1. Trace Blue Cat and Circle

front-and-back patterns, page 69. Make a template for each pattern.
2. On *right* side of one layer of white print, trace Circle template for front. Stack print pieces and cut out together, adding a ¼" seam allowance.
3. Prepare and cut Blue Cat appliqué for either hand or machine stitching.
4. Center cat on right side of front circle and sew in place.
5. Add embroidery lines in white.
6. Prepare padding, quilt and finish potholder; see *To make a potholder,* opposite page.

PEACH PIG

Fig. 4 Peach Pig *(color photo, page 11)*

Cut out the appliqué in one piece and add black lines for the head and tail.

Materials

2 squares green print fabric, 8x8" each, for front and back
peach fabric, 7x7", for pig
lightweight, fusible interfacing, 7x7" (for machine appliqué)
3 squares terry cloth, 8x8" each, for padding
28" green double-fold bias binding, ¼" wide

thread for stitching and quilting
black embroidery floss or
thread, for embroidery lines

Directions

See *General guides for appliqué,*
page 2.

1. Trace Peach Pig pattern,
page 70, and Circle front-and-
back pattern (shown with Blue
Cat), page 69. Make a template
for each pattern.
2. On *right* side of one layer of
green print, trace Circle template for front. Stack print
pieces and cut out together,
adding a ¼″ seam allowance.
3. Prepare and cut Peach Pig
appliqué for either hand or
machine stitching.
4. Center pig on right side of
front circle and sew in place.
5. Add embroidery lines in
black.
6. Prepare padding, quilt and
finish potholder; see *To make a
potholder,* page 62.

WHITE HEN

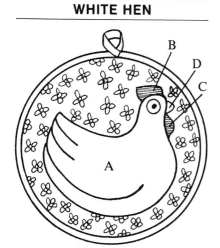

Fig. 5 White Hen
(color photo, page 11)

The combination of blue and
white gives this design a clean,
country look.

Materials

2 squares blue print fabric, 8x8″
each, for front and back
white fabric, 7x7″, for hen
red scrap, for comb and wattle
yellow scrap, for beak
lightweight, fusible interfacing,
7x9″ (for machine appliqué)
3 squares terry cloth, 8x8″ each,
for padding
28″ blue double-fold bias bind-
ing, ¼″ wide
thread for stitching and quilting
dark blue embroidery floss or
thread, for embroidery lines

Directions

See *General guides for appliqué,*
page 2.

1. Trace White Hen pattern,
page 70, and Circle front-and-
back pattern (shown with Blue
Cat), page 69. Make a template
for A-D of hen and for Circle.
2. On *right* side of one layer of
blue print, trace Circle template
for front. Stack blue print
pieces and cut out together,
adding a ¼″ seam allowance.
3. Prepare and cut appliqué
pieces for either hand or machine stitching. Use white for A,
red for B (comb) and C (wattle),
and yellow for D (beak).
4. Center appliqué pieces on
right side of front circle and sew
in place.
5. Add embroidery lines in blue.
6. Prepare padding, quilt and
finish potholder; see *To make a
potholder,* page 62.

Fig. 6 Question Mark
(color photo, page 11)

Let this potholder ask "What's
cooking?"

Materials

2 squares yellow print fabric,
8x8″ each, for front and back
red fabric, 6x8″, for design
lightweight, fusible interfacing,
6x8″ (for machine appliqué)
3 squares terry cloth, 8x8″ each,
for padding
28″ yellow double-fold bias
binding, ¼″ wide
thread for stitching and quilting

Directions

See *General guides for appliqué,*
page 2.

1. Trace pattern pieces A and B
for Question Mark, page 71,
and pattern for Circle front-
and-back (shown with Blue
Cat), page 69. Make a template
for each piece.
2. On *right* side of one layer of
yellow print, trace Circle template for front. Stack print
pieces and cut out together,
adding a ¼″ seam allowance.
3. Prepare and cut appliqué
pieces for either hand or machine stitching, using red fabric.
4. Center Question Mark on

right side of front circle and sew in place.

5. Prepare padding, quilt and finish potholder; see *To make a potholder*, page 62.

TULIP

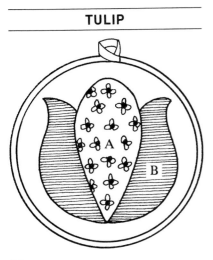

Fig. 7 Tulip
(color photo, page 11)

Use two fabrics for this design with a folk-art look.

Materials

*2 squares white fabric, 8x8"
  each, for front and back
yellow print, 4x7", for design
red fabric, 7x7", for design
lightweight, fusible interfacing,
  7x11" (for machine appliqué)
3 squares terry cloth, 8x8" each,
  for padding
28" red double-fold bias binding, ¼" wide
thread for stitching and quilting*

Directions

See *General guides for appliqué*, page 2.

1. Trace Tulip pattern, page 71, and Circle front-and-back pattern (shown with Blue Cat), page 69. Make a template for A and B of Tulip and for Circle.
2. On *right* side of one layer of white fabric, trace Circle template for front. Stack white pieces and cut out together,

adding a ¼" seam allowance.
3. Prepare and cut appliqué pieces for either hand or machine stitching. Use yellow print for one A piece and red for one B and one B-reversed piece.
4. Center appliqué pieces on right side of front circle and sew in place.
5. Prepare padding, quilt and finish potholder; see *To make a potholder*, page 62.

RAINBOW

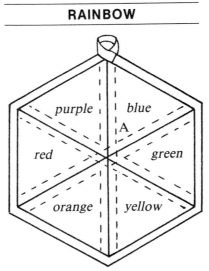

Fig. 8 Rainbow
(color photo, page 11)

Use six different colors and one pattern piece for this simple pieced work design.

Materials

*6 squares fabric (purple, blue,
  green, yellow, orange, red),
  5x5½" each
print fabric, 9x10", for back
3 pieces terry cloth, 9x10" each,
  for padding
33" yellow double-fold bias
  binding, ¼" wide
thread for stitching; white
  thread for quilting*

Directions

See *General guides for pieced work*, page 5.

1. Trace patterns for Rainbow

A, page 72, and Hexagon Back, page 73. Make a template for each pattern.
2. Place templates on *wrong* side of fabric. On each color, trace one A. On print, trace one Hexagon Back. Cut out, adding a ¼" seam allowance.
3. Lay triangles flat, right side up, to form design in Fig. 8.
4. Pin two triangles together. Begin stitching at outside raw edge, and stop exactly on the seam line at center of design; do not stitch into the seam allowance. Add one more triangle in the same manner to complete half the design. Press all seam allowances flat and in the same direction; trim to ⅛".

Repeat to complete other half of design. Join the two halves, making sure all points meet at center. (You may want to baste center area before stitching.) Press seam, and trim to ⅛".
5. Prepare padding, quilt and finish potholder; see *To make a potholder*, page 62. To quilt Rainbow (Step 3), use white thread, and stitch ¼" from each seam (see Fig. 8).

HEXAGON BEAUTY

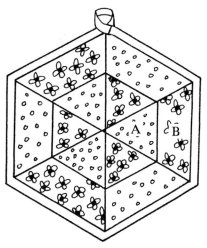

Fig. 9 Hexagon Beauty
(color photo, page 11)

Here's a traditional quilt block done in potholder size.

Materials
brown fabric with white dots, 10x16", for design and back
second brown print, 7x10", for design
3 pieces terry cloth, 9x10" each, for padding
33" orange double-fold bias binding, ¼" wide
thread for stitching and quilting

Directions
See *General guides for pieced work*, page 5.
1. Trace pattern pieces A and B for Hexagon Beauty, page 72, and Hexagon Back, page 73. Make a template for each piece.
2. Place templates on *wrong* side of fabric. On brown fabric with white dots, trace three A, three B and one Back. On second brown print, trace three A and three B pieces. Cut out, adding a ¼" seam allowance.
3. Lay pieces flat, right side up, to form design in Fig. 9. Join each A to a B to form a large triangle. Join large triangles,

following directions for Step 4 under Rainbow, page 65.
4. Prepare padding, quilt and finish potholder; see *To make a potholder*, page 62.

DIAMOND STAR

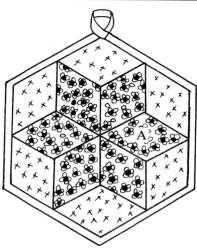

Fig. 10 Diamond Star
(color photo, page 11)

All pieces for this potholder design are cut from one pattern. Six red print diamonds, forming the center star, are surrounded by six yellow print diamonds.

Materials
yellow print fabric, 9x18", for design and back
red print, 8x8", for design
3 pieces terry cloth, 9x10" each, for padding
33" red double-fold bias binding, ¼" wide
thread for stitching and quilting

Directions
See *General guides for pieced work*, page 5.
1. Trace patterns for Diamond Star A, page 72, and Hexagon Back, page 73. Make a template for each pattern.
2. Place templates on *wrong* side of fabric. On yellow print, trace six A pieces and one Back.

On red print, trace six A pieces. Cut out, adding a ¼" seam allowance.
3. Lay pieces flat, right side up, to form design in Fig. 10, with red print diamonds forming the center star. Join two red print A pieces, stitching only on the seam (pencil) line; do not stitch into seam allowances. Add one more red print A to complete half the star. Press all seams flat and in the same direction, and trim to ⅛".

Repeat to complete other half of star, then join the two halves.

Add yellow print A pieces, stitching one side at a time. With yellow print A on the bottom, stitch from outside raw edge to end of seam (pencil) line; do not stitch into seam allowance. Rearrange fabric, and stitch from end of seam line to outside raw edge.
4. Prepare padding, quilt and finish potholder; see *To make a potholder*, page 62.

SHADOW BOX

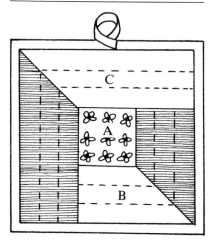

Fig. 11 Shadow Box
(color photo, page 11)

Two solid colors and one print create this shadow box effect.

Materials

orange print fabric, 8x12", for design and back (or ¼ yd., if you also make matching bias binding)
white fabric, 7x8", for design
orange fabric, 7x8", for design
3 pieces terry cloth, 9x10" each, for padding
1 yd. orange double-fold bias binding, ¼" wide (if you purchase bias)
thread for stitching; orange thread for quilting

Directions

See *General guides for pieced work*, page 5. If you wish to make bias binding, see page 6.

1. Trace pattern pieces A-C and Back for Shadow Box, pages 67-68. Make a template for each piece.

2. Place templates on *wrong* side of fabric. On orange print, trace one A and one Back. On white, trace one B and one C piece. On orange, trace one B-reversed and one C-reversed piece. Cut out, adding a ¼" seam allowance.

3. Lay pieces flat, right side up, to form design in Fig. 11. Join white B to center A, stitching from raw edge of straight side to end of seam (pencil) line at diagonal (Fig. 12). Join orange B (reversed) to A in same manner. Then join the two B pieces to close the diagonal seam.

   Repeat to attach the two C pieces.

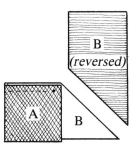

Fig. 12 *Joining B pieces to center A*

4. Prepare padding, quilt and finish potholder; see *To make a potholder*, page 62. To quilt Shadow Box, see Fig. 11. Mark two parallel quilting lines on the B and C pieces, dividing pieces into three equal parts. Stitch lines with orange thread.

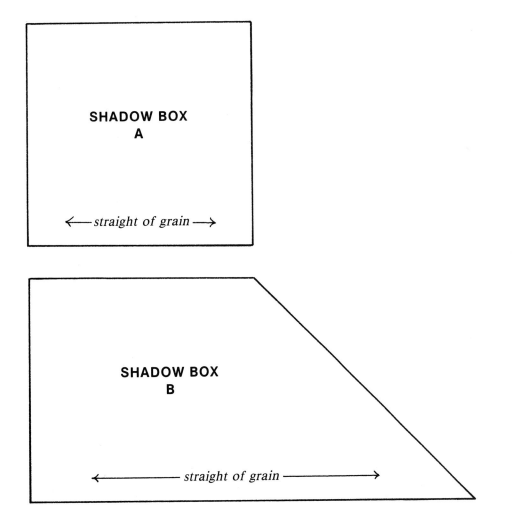

SHADOW BOX
A

←— straight of grain —→

SHADOW BOX
B

←——— straight of grain ———→

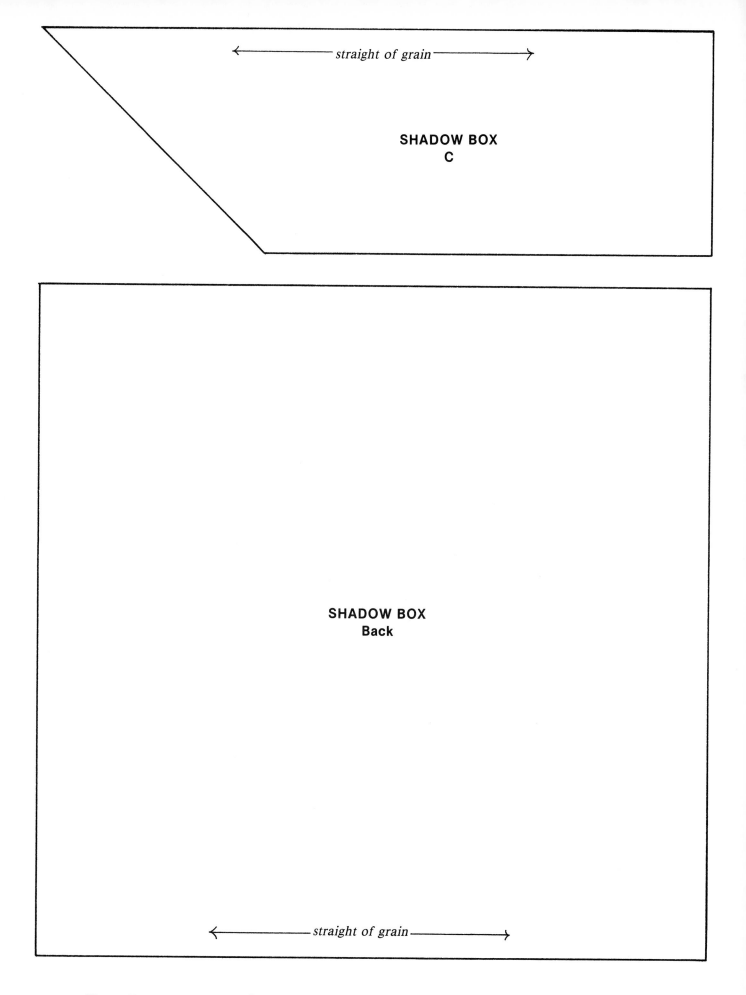

SHADOW BOX
C

straight of grain

SHADOW BOX
Back

straight of grain

short broken lines are embroidery lines

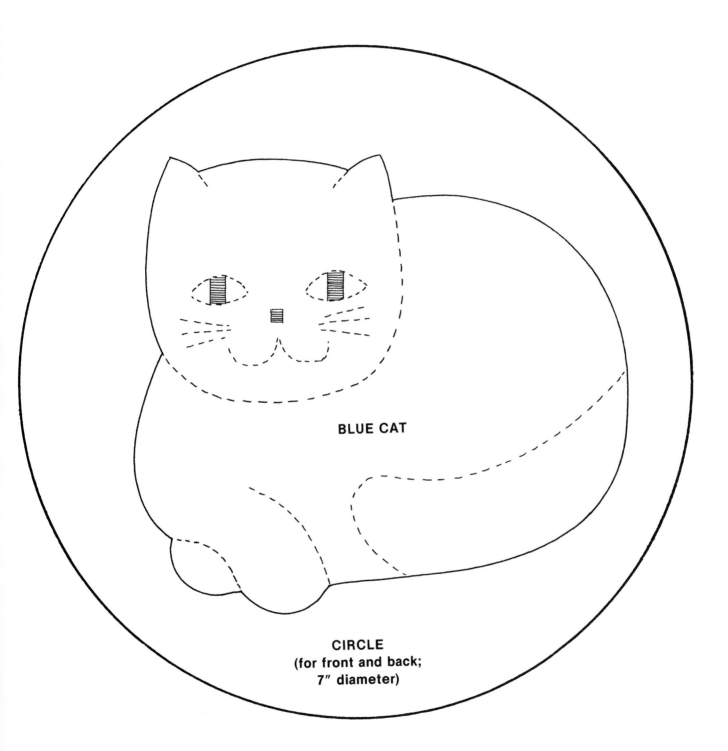

BLUE CAT

CIRCLE
(for front and back;
7" diameter)

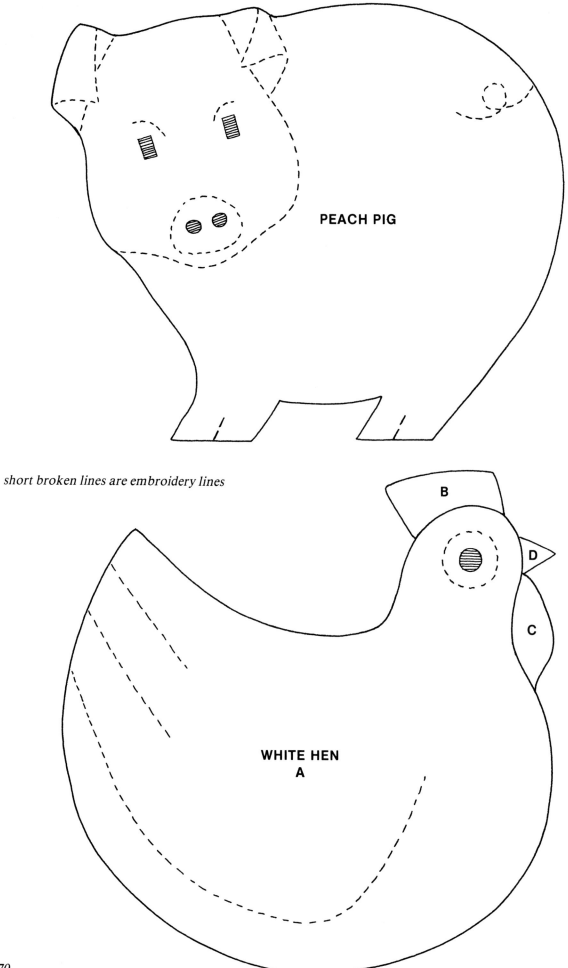

PEACH PIG

short broken lines are embroidery lines

**WHITE HEN
A**

B

D

C

70

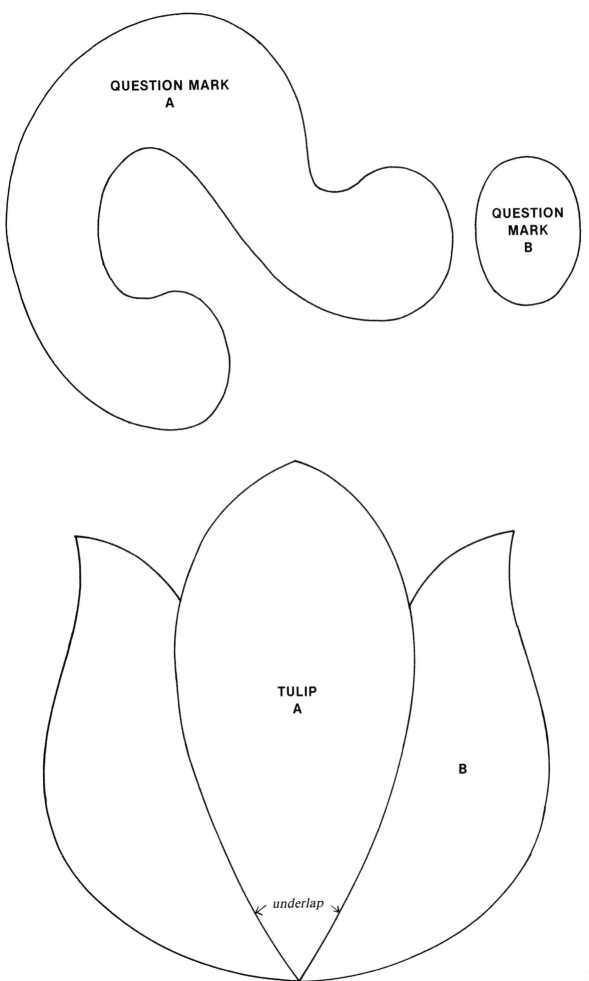

QUESTION MARK
A

QUESTION
MARK
B

TULIP
A

B

underlap

71

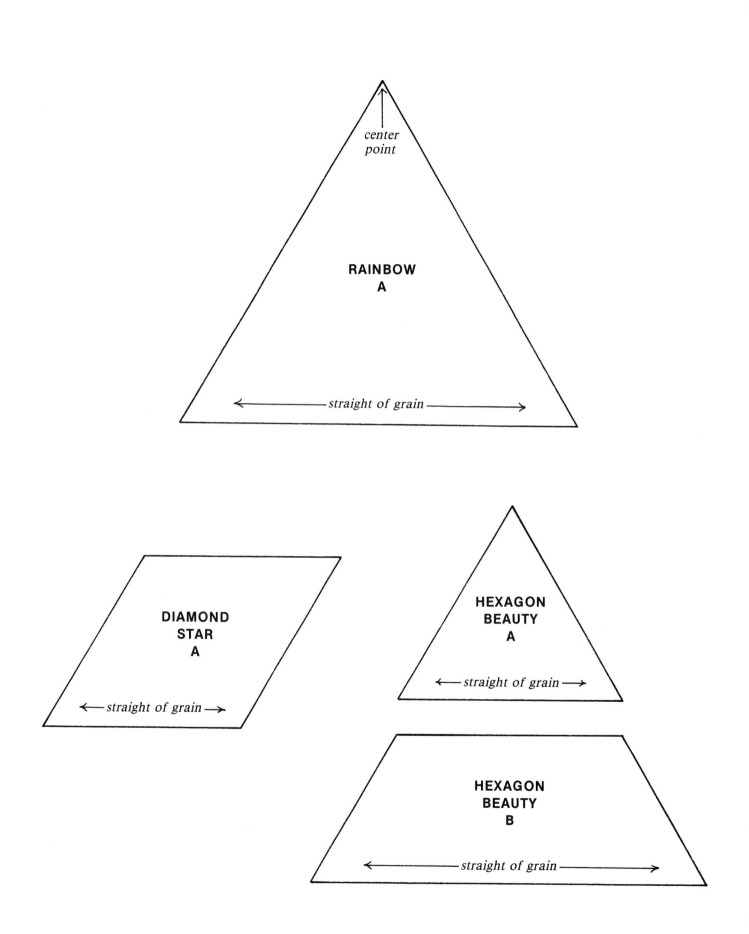

RAINBOW
A

center
point

straight of grain

DIAMOND
STAR
A

straight of grain

HEXAGON
BEAUTY
A

straight of grain

HEXAGON
BEAUTY
B

straight of grain

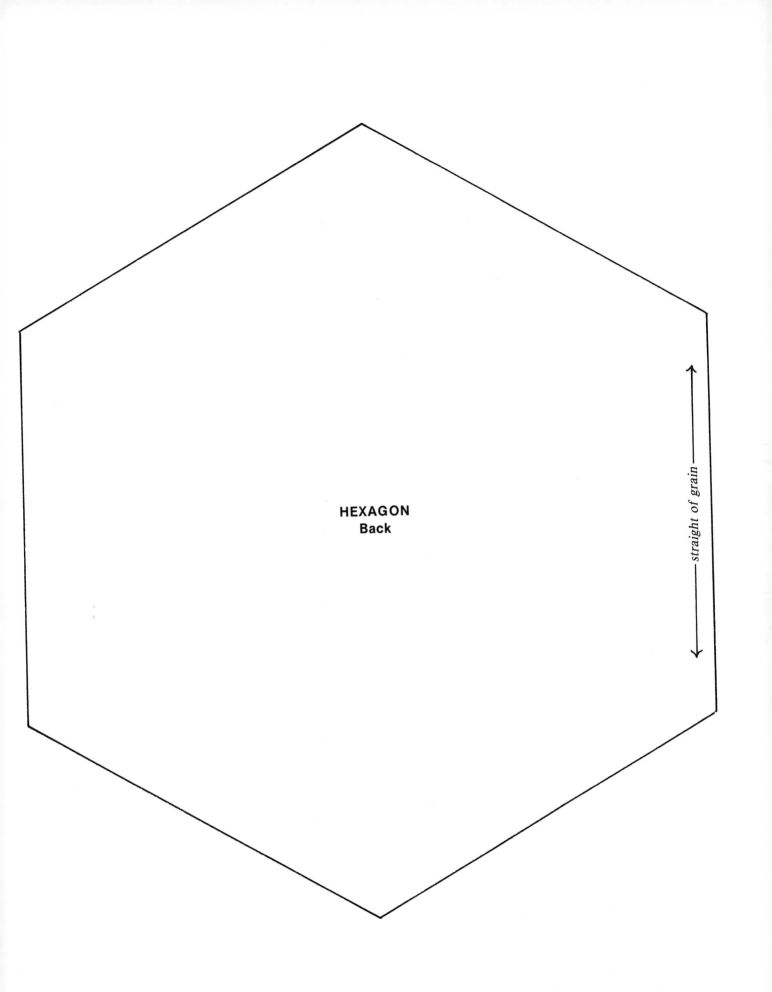

HEXAGON
Back

straight of grain

6

Crib quilts

Here are four appliqué designs created especially for crib quilts. You can set the blocks together without sashing. Finish the edges with bias quilt binding or a fold-over border like the one shown on our Floating Clown quilt, page 84.

These patterns aren't limited to quilts, of course. You can use one Little Bear block for a pillow top, as we did; our sample is shown on page 84. Add a 1″ border to make it 14″ square, and cut a pillow back and other layers to fit (see *To make a pillow,* page 7). Or use the two blocks of the Floating Clown design as a rectangular wall hanging.

To make quilts in other patterns, you could use the Big Sun or the Peeping Cat (without the rug), page 30. Appliqué the designs to 13½″-square blocks and follow directions for the Fish in the Sea quilt, page 75.

Materials and directions are given for making large crib quilts, about 40x60″. To make a shorter quilt, you can omit a row of blocks. To make a larger quilt for an older child, just add more blocks to increase both width and length.

To make a crib quilt

1. Complete quilt top, following directions for the pattern you choose.

2. Quilt layers; see *General guides for quilting,* page 5. First, decide on quilting lines. You may want to quilt around each appliqué to emphasize it.

If the appliqué blocks are set between other blocks that have no appliqué, do some quilting inside the plain blocks. You can repeat part or all of the appliqué pattern, or just quilt inside the edges of the blocks. On busy prints, keep the design simple—stitches won't show up well.

A quick method of quilting is to stitch around each block, on top of the seam line, as we did on the Fish in the Sea quilt, page 85.

If any guidelines are needed for quilting, mark them on the quilt top with a sharp pencil.

Stack layers, centering each one, in this order: back, right side down; batting; quilt top (front), right side up. Baste to hold in place; sew from center to outside edges and then around edges. Keep all layers

smooth.

Note: If batting is too short, add a strip cut from the side. Butt edges together and catch with loose hand stitches.

Quilt the layers by hand or machine.

3. Finish edge with bias or a fold-over border. (To make your own bias, see page 6.)

For a bias binding, first machine-stitch binding to quilt top. Place fold line of bias over seam line of quilt, right sides together, and stitch along the fold line. You can round corners gently, or you can make them square by mitering the

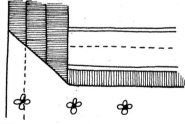

Fig. 1 *Adding bias and beginning miter*

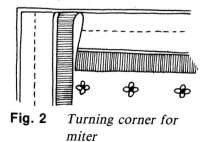

Fig. 2 *Turning corner for miter*

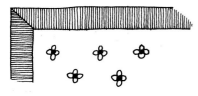

Fig. 3 *Bias folded over edge*

corners (Figs. 1-3) or by binding each side separately.

For a fold-over border, the back fabric must be 3″ wider and longer than the quilt front, so it extends 1½″ beyond front on all sides.

Trim batting to match quilt front. To miter each corner, fold fabric diagonally across corner, onto quilt top (Fig. 4). Fold back fabric onto top along edges (Fig. 5), forming miter at corner. Turn raw edges under, making a ¾″ border. Clip off raw edge of exposed corner (Fig. 6).

Baste border in place. By hand, sew edges of miter together. By hand or machine, sew border to quilt top.

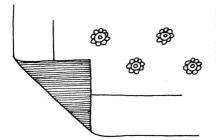

Fig. 4 *Folding corner diagonally to begin fold-over border*

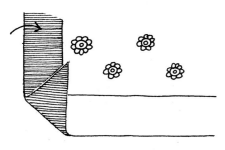
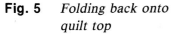

Fig. 5 *Folding back onto quilt top*

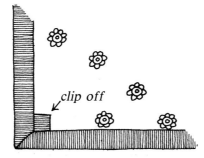

Fig. 6 *Finishing fold-over border*

FISH IN THE SEA

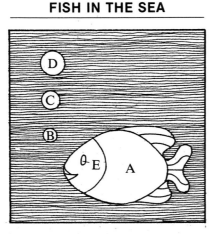

Fig. 7 Fish in the Sea
(color photo, page 85)

Red fish swim through a royal blue sea, blowing red bubbles. Eight fish blocks are set with blue fabric blocks between them, and red bias binds the edge. You can appliqué the eyes as we did, or embroider them with a satin stitch. Blocks are 12″ square, and the finished quilt is 37½x61½″.

Materials
3½ yd. royal blue fabric with white dots, 44″ wide, for blocks and back
½ yd. red fabric with white dots, 44″ wide, for design
1 yd. lightweight, fusible interfacing, 22″ wide (for machine appliqué)
1 pkg. polyester batting, crib quilt size (45x60″)

6 yd. red bias quilt binding, ¾″ wide
thread for stitching and quilting
blue embroidery floss or thread, for embroidery lines

Directions
See *General guides for appliqué,* page 2.
1. Trace pattern pieces A-E for Fish in the Sea, page 79. Make a template for each piece.
2. On *wrong* side of blue fabric, mark and cut one 37½x61½″ piece for back, and 15 blocks, 13½x13½″ each. Measurements include ¾″ seam allowances.
3. Prepare and cut appliqué pieces for either hand or machine stitching. Use red for eight A, eight B, eight C and eight D pieces. Use blue for eight E pieces.
4. Position appliqué pieces on right side of blue blocks (bubbles are 1″ apart), and sew in place. Add embroidery lines in blue.
5. Arrange blocks as in Fig. 8, with fabric blocks separating the

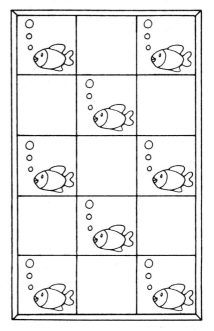

Fig. 8 *Layout for Fish in the Sea crib quilt*

eight appliquéd blocks.

6. Machine-stitch blocks, right sides together, to form five horizontal rows. Stitch ¾″ seams, then trim to ¼″.

Join rows to complete quilt top. Stitch ¾″ seams, then trim to ¼″. Leave all seam allowances on the outside edge the full ¾″; these will be covered with bias. Stitch around outside edge, directly over seam line; this transfers seam line to right side.

7. Quilt layers and finish edge; see *To make a crib quilt*, page 74. Bind edge with red bias quilt binding.

LITTLE BEAR

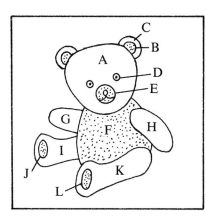

Fig. 9 Little Bear
(*color photo, page 84*)

A single bear looks great on a pillow top, but eight bears on a quilt look even better. Set the blocks like the Fish in the Sea quilt, page 75, with print blocks between the appliqués. Blocks are 12″ square and the finished quilt is 37½x61½″.

Materials

3¼ yd. peach with brown print fabric, 44″ wide, for design, quilt blocks and back
1¼ yd. ecru fabric, 44″ wide, for appliqué blocks
⅝ yd. brown fabric, 44″ wide, for design
1¾ yd. lightweight, fusible interfacing, 22″ wide (for machine appliqué)
1 pkg. polyester batting, crib quilt size (45x60″)
6 yd. brown bias quilt binding, ¾″ wide
thread for stitching and quilting
black embroidery floss or thread, for embroidery lines

Directions

See *General guides for appliqué*, page 2.

1. Trace pattern for Little Bear, pages 80-81. Make a template for each piece, A-L.

2. On *wrong* side of print fabric, mark and cut one 37½x61½″ back, and seven blocks, 13½x13½″ each.

On *wrong* side of ecru fabric, mark and cut eight blocks, 13½x13½″ each. All the measurements include ¾″ seam allowances.

3. Prepare and cut appliqué pieces for either hand or machine stitching. Use print for eight B, eight B-reversed, 16 D, eight E, eight F, eight J and eight L pieces. Use brown for eight A, eight C, eight C-reversed, eight G, eight H, eight I and eight K pieces.

4. Position appliqué pieces on right side of ecru blocks, and sew in place. Where pieces overlap, sew bottom layer first.

Add embroidery lines. Stitch nose, mouth and eye pupils in black.

5. Arrange blocks as in Fig. 8

(Fish in the Sea), page 75, alternating Little Bear appliqués with blocks of print fabric.

Join blocks, following Step 6 of Fish in the Sea.

6. Quilt layers and finish edge; see *To make a crib quilt*, page 74. Bind edge with brown bias quilt binding.

FLOATING CLOWN

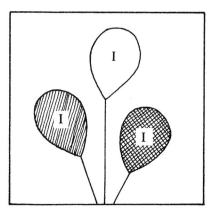

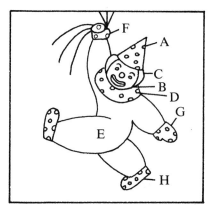

Fig 10 Floating Clown
(*color photo, page 84*)

Seven happy clowns float in space with their colorful balloons. Three solid colors and one print form the design, and blue thread outlines all pieces except face and hair. The print is also used for the back, which folds over the edge to form a border. Blocks are 12″ square and the finished quilt is 37½x61½″.

Materials

1 ¾ yd. white fabric, 44" wide, for quilt blocks and clown faces

½ yd. yellow-gold fabric, 44" wide, for clowns and balloons

2 ¼ yd. yellow and blue print, 44" wide, for design and quilt back

orange fabric, 9x22", for hair and balloons

blue fabric, 9x18", for balloons

1 ⅞ yd. lightweight, fusible interfacing, 22" wide (for machine appliqué)

1 pkg. polyester batting, crib quilt size (45x60")

thread for stitching and quilting

blue, orange and black embroidery floss or thread, for embroidery lines

Directions

See *General guides for appliqué,* page 2.

1. Trace patterns for Floating Clown (including balloons), pages 82 and 87. Make a template for each piece, A-I.

2. On *wrong* side of white fabric, mark and cut 12 blocks, 13½ x13½" each. Measurements include ¾" seam allowances.

From print, cut a 40½ x64½" back (this includes 3" extra on both length and width for fold-over border).

3. Prepare and cut appliqué pieces for either hand or machine stitching. Use yellow-gold for seven E and eight I pieces. Use print for seven A, seven D, seven F, seven G and 14 H pieces. Use orange for seven C (hair), seven C-reversed and eight I pieces. Use blue for eight I pieces.

Use white for seven B (face) pieces; transfer inside design lines. If you are doing machine appliqué, you may wish to stitch embroidery lines on faces before cutting them out. Use orange for nose and mouth, blue for eyes and black for eyebrows.

4. Position appliqué pieces on right side of white blocks, and transfer embroidery lines for balloon strings (these will be extended later).

Sew appliqués in place. Where pieces overlap, sew bottom layer first. On our sample quilt, faces and hair were appliquéd with matching thread. All other appliqué pieces were stitched in blue.

Embroider faces if you have not already done so. (For colors to use, see Step 3.)

5. Arrange blocks as in Fig. 11. Machine-stitch each clown block to the balloon block above it, right sides together. Stitch ¾" seams, then trim to ¼".

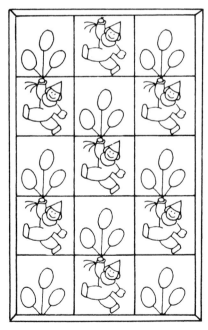

Fig. 11 *Layout for Floating Clown crib quilt*

With pencil, connect lines that run from each clown's hand to the balloons above him. Embroider lines in blue.

6. Machine-stitch blocks, right sides together, to form three vertical rows. Stitch ¾" seams, then trim to ¼".

Join rows to complete quilt top. Stitch ¾" seams, then trim to ¼". Leave all seam allowances on the outside edge the full ¾"; these will be covered by the fold-over border. Stitch around outside edge, directly over seam line; this transfers seam line to right side.

7. Quilt layers and finish edge; see *To make a crib quilt,* page 74. Use a fold-over border to finish the edge.

PAPER DOLLS

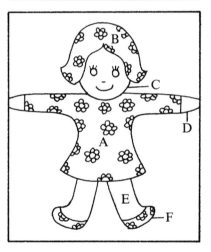

Fig. 12 Paper Dolls
(color photo, page 84)

Remember when you folded paper to cut a row of dolls—and the dolls were holding hands when you unfolded them? This version is done in fabric. There is a row of girls, then a row of boys, and each doll has a different combination of print and plain fabrics. (You could use just one solid color and two prints.) A green border frames the blocks, and the edge is bound in bias. Blocks are 10x12″ and the finished quilt is 42x60″.

Materials

1¼ yd. white fabric, 44″ wide, for quilt blocks

2 yd. print fabric, 44″ wide, for back and design

1 yd. light green fabric, 44″ wide, for border

12 pieces of fabric, 7x14″ each, in a variety of prints, for dolls

12 pieces of fabric, 6x8″ each, in a variety of solid colors, for dolls

2¼ yd. lightweight, fusible interfacing, 22″ wide (for machine appliqué)

1 pkg. polyester batting, crib quilt size (45x60″)

6 yd. green bias quilt binding, ¾″ wide

thread for stitching and quilting

black embroidery floss or thread, for embroidery lines

Directions

See *General guides for appliqué,* page 2.

1. Draw a 10x12″ rectangle on tracing paper and fold it in half down the 12″ length. Open paper and place it over pattern for Girl, page 88, with paper fold on broken line. Trace half the pattern.

Refold paper, with traced sec-tion on the bottom, and copy pattern onto other half of paper.

Use another sheet of tracing paper to trace pattern for Boy, page 89, in the same manner.

Make a template for each pattern piece, A-F (for Girl) and G-L (for Boy).

2. On *wrong* side of white fabric, mark and cut 12 blocks, 10½x12½″ each. Measurements include ¼″ seam allowances.

From the large piece of print fabric, cut a 42x60″ quilt back.

3. Prepare and cut appliqué pieces for either hand or machine stitching. Cut pieces for six girls and six boys.

For each doll: From print, cut one garment (A or G), one hair (B or H) and two shoes (F or L), reversing one shoe piece. From solid color, cut one face (C or I), two hands (D or J) and two legs (E or K), reversing one leg piece.

For either hand or machine work, add a ¼″ seam allowance to the end of each hand; this will be caught in the seam when blocks are stitched together.

4. Position appliqué pieces on right side of white block, and sew in place. Where pieces overlap, sew bottom layer first.

Add embroidery lines to faces in black. Outline eyes; do not fill in centers.

5. Arrange blocks as in Fig. 13. Join blocks to form four horizontal rows, then join the rows. Stitch ¼″ seams.

6. Add border. From light green fabric, cut two strips 6¼x42″ each, for top and bottom. Cut two strips 6¼x41½″ each, and two strips, 6¼x7½″ each, for sides. (Sides must be pieced, but quilting lines will hide seams.)

Sew each long side strip to a

short side strip, right sides together, with a ¼″ seam; this forms a strip 6¼x48½″.

Add a side border strip to each side of quilt top, with pieced seam near bottom; stitch ¼″ seams. Add top and bottom border strips.

7. Quilt layers and finish edge; see *To make a crib quilt,* page 74. To quilt side borders, extend lines from doll hands, sewing from edge of quilt blocks to outside edge of border; this will cover pieced seams.

To quilt top and bottom borders, find center of each block and sew from edge of block to outside edge of border.

Finish edge with green bias quilt binding, using ¾″ (width of bias) for seam allowance.

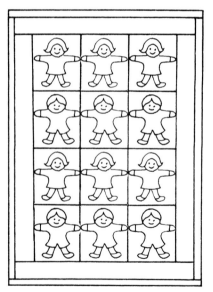

Fig. 13 *Layout for Paper Dolls crib quilt*

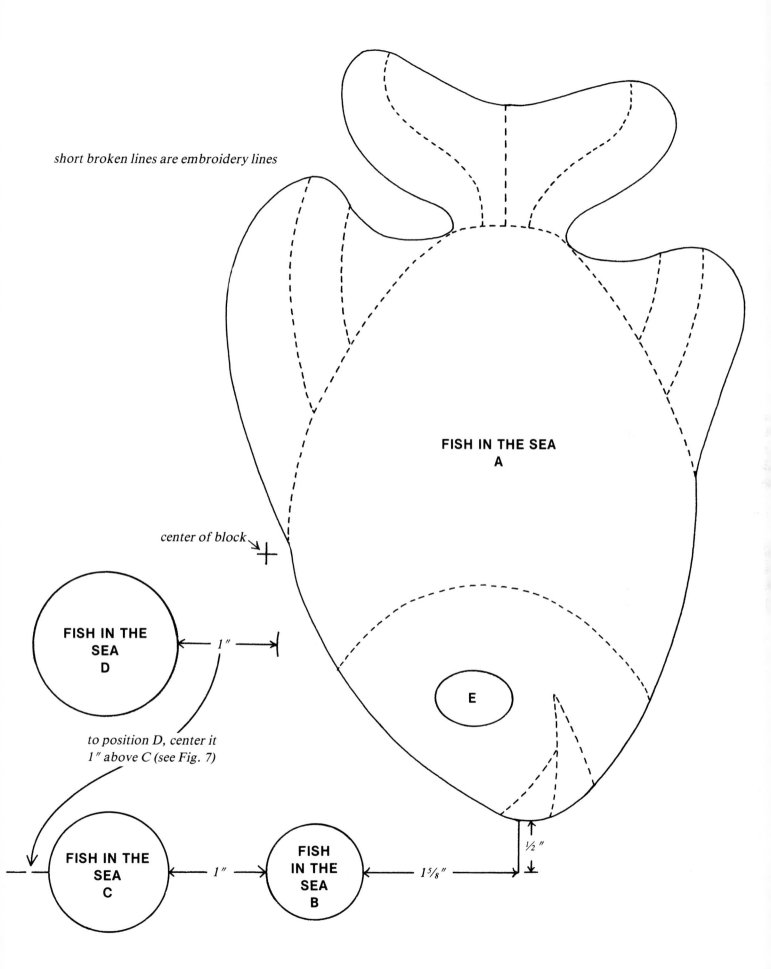

short broken lines are embroidery lines

**FISH IN THE SEA
A**

center of block ↘ +

**FISH IN THE
SEA
D**

← *1″* →

*to position D, center it
1″ above C (see Fig. 7)*

**FISH IN THE
SEA
C**

← *1″* →

**FISH
IN THE
SEA
B**

← *1⅝″* →

½″

E

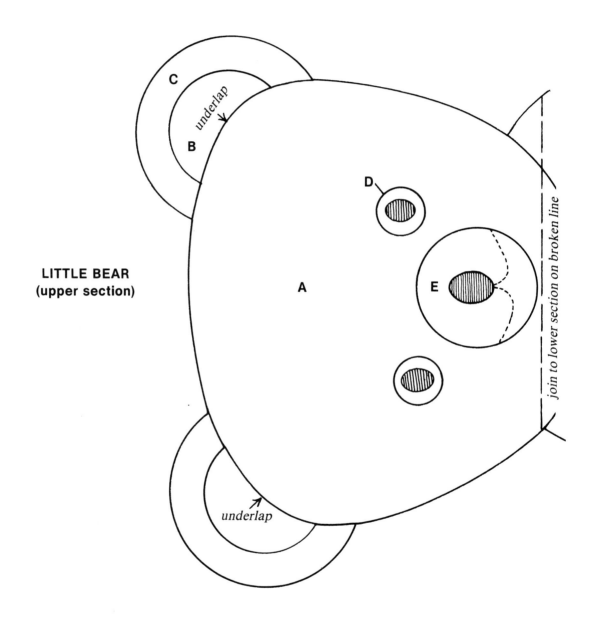

LITTLE BEAR
(upper section)

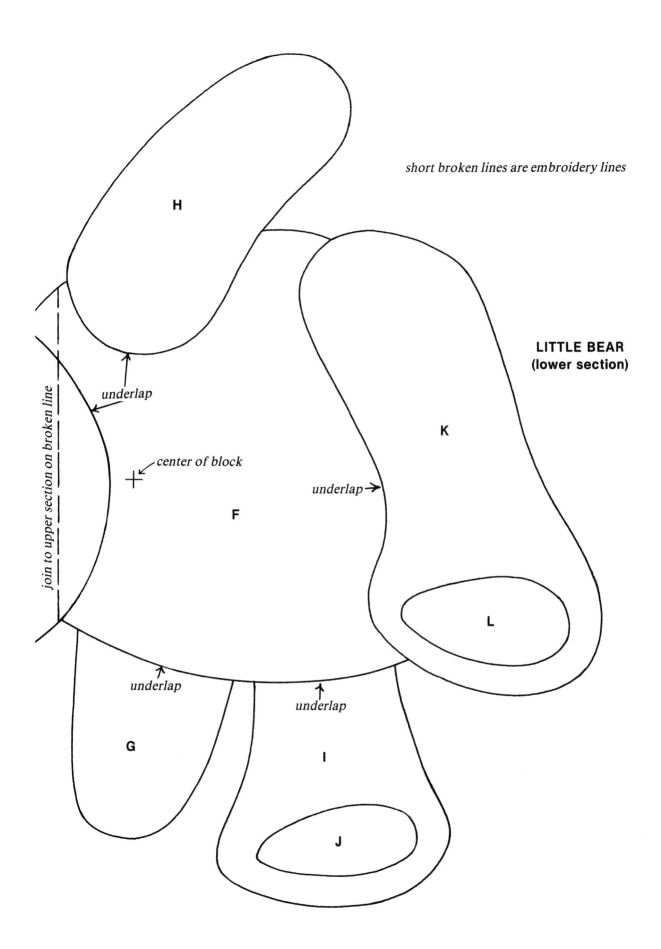

short broken lines are embroidery lines

H

LITTLE BEAR
(lower section)

underlap

join to upper section on broken line

center of block

F

underlap

K

L

underlap

underlap

G

I

J

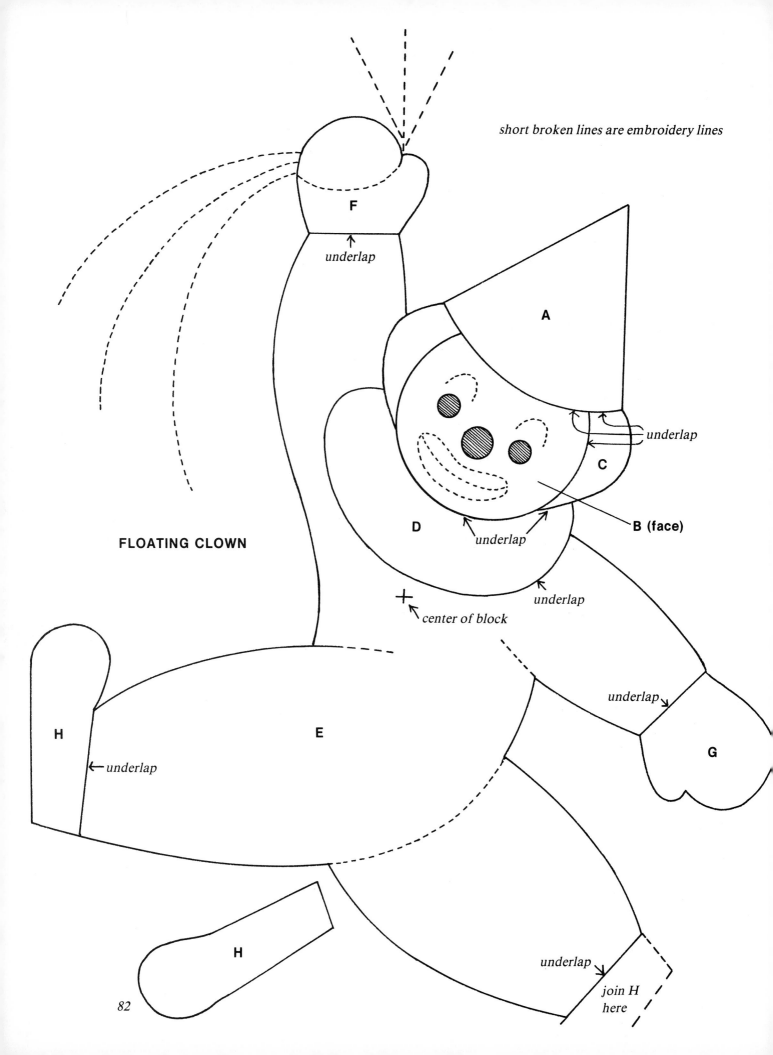

short broken lines are embroidery lines

F

underlap

A

underlap

C

B (face)

D

underlap

underlap

center of block

FLOATING CLOWN

E

H

underlap

underlap

G

H

underlap

join H
here

82

Make a bib or small handbag and add an appliqué—Chapter 7 has all the directions. Appliqué patterns shown on these bibs are the Butterfly (page 96), Pink Bow (page 96), and Bow Tie and Collar (page 96). On the shoulder bags, left to right, are the Four-Leaf Clover (page 97), Stack of Hearts (page 97) and the Folded Rose (page 3l), which is borrowed from a tote bag design.

Delight a youngster with a crib quilt, using one of these special designs. Patterns are, left to right, Floating Clown (page 76); Paper Dolls (page 77); Little Bear, shown above as a pillow top (page 76); and Fish in the Sea (page 75).

Dress up plain, ready-made clothes with appliqués. Designs on the small shirts at left, from top to bottom, are the Blue Ribbon (page 96), Elephant (page 97), and Whale (page 99). The white T-shirt at center displays a Flat Rose with long stem (page 99). On the toddler's clothing at right, top to bottom, are the Strawberry (page 99), small hearts from Stack of Hearts (page 97) and Minnow (page 98).

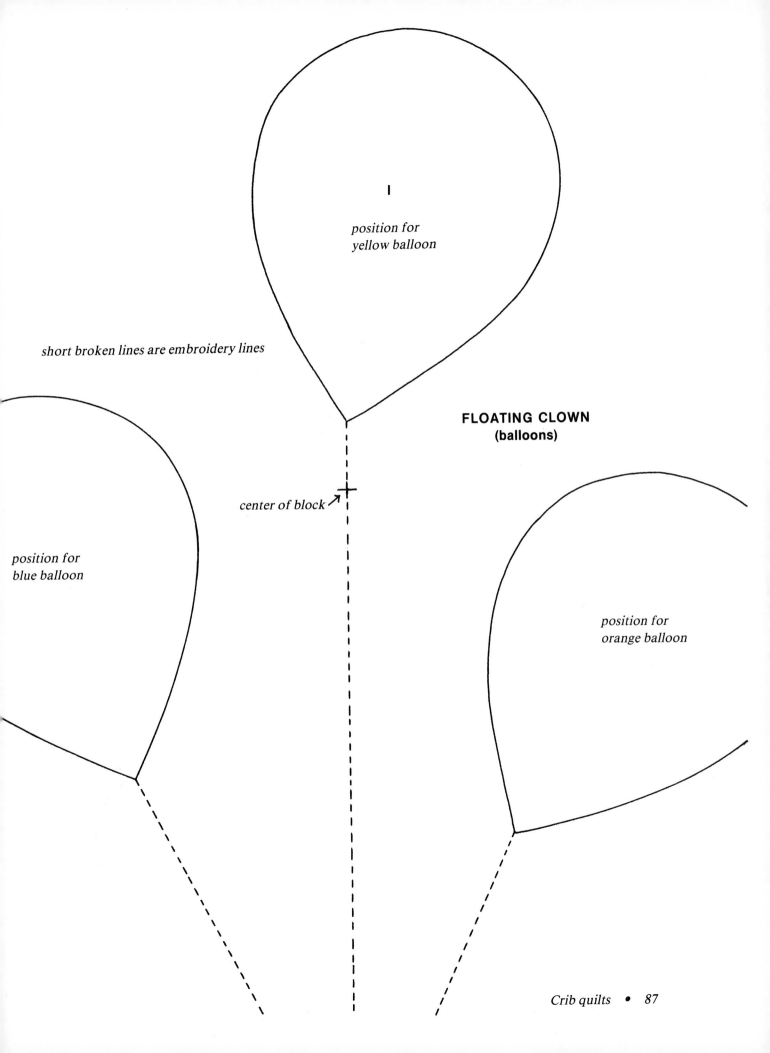

position for
yellow balloon

short broken lines are embroidery lines

FLOATING CLOWN
(balloons)

center of block ↗

position for
blue balloon

position for
orange balloon

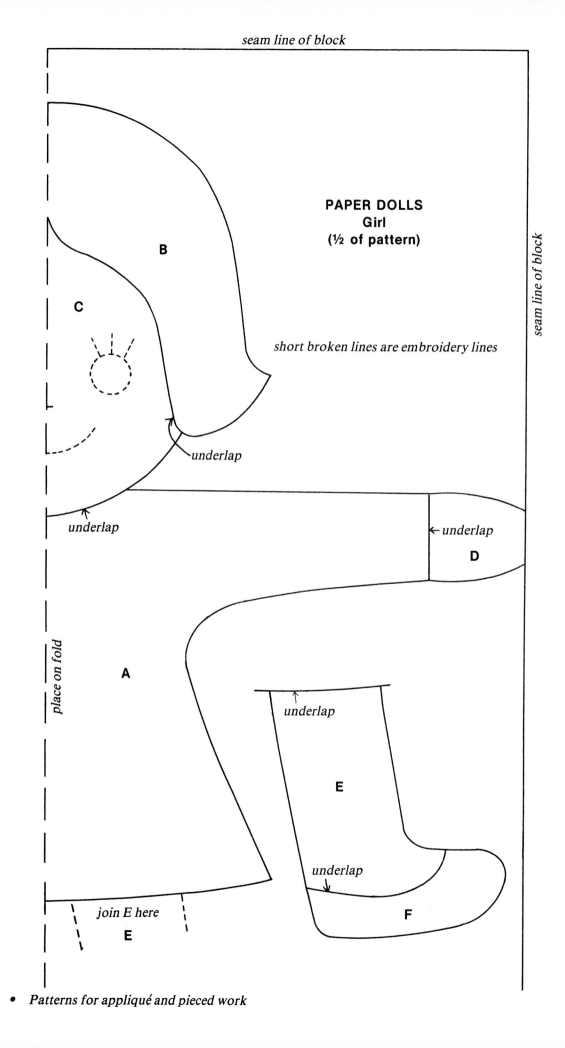

seam line of block

seam line of block

PAPER DOLLS
Girl
(½ of pattern)

B

C

short broken lines are embroidery lines

underlap

underlap

← underlap

D

place on fold

A

underlap

E

underlap

F

join E here

E

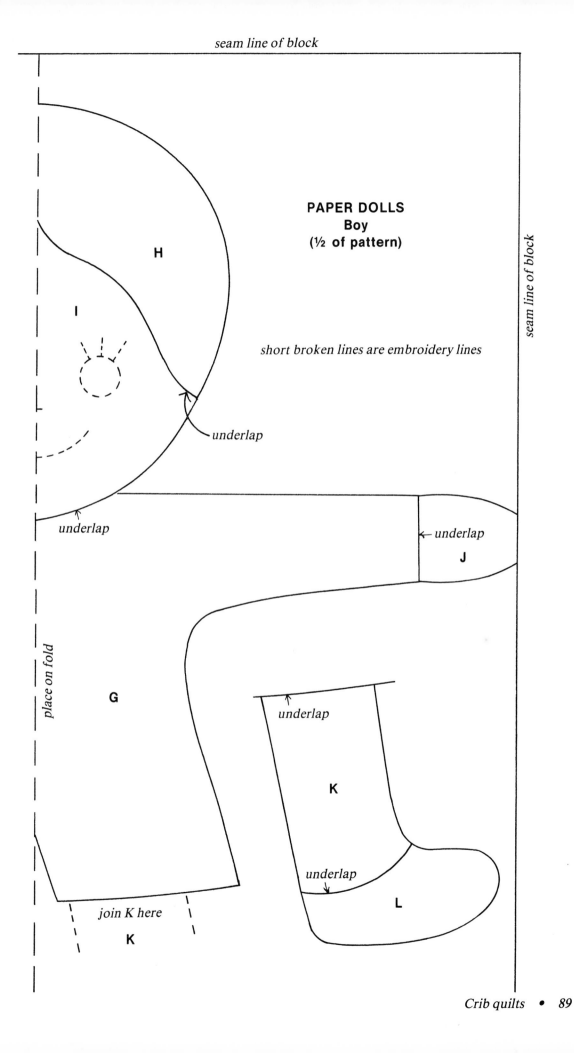

seam line of block

PAPER DOLLS
Boy
(½ of pattern)

H

I

short broken lines are embroidery lines

underlap

underlap

seam line of block

underlap

J

place on fold

G

underlap

K

underlap

join K here

K

L

7

Designs to wear

In this chapter, you'll find more than 30 appliqué patterns to decorate clothes for children and adults. Stitch the designs to shirts, jackets, vests, dresses, aprons, slacks and jeans. Use them on pockets, too—and as patches. (Who would guess the little red apple is covering a tear in your toddler's overalls?)

Let one minnow appliqué "swim" alone on a blouse collar, or make a border of them for a skirt. Sew a row of graduated hearts up one leg of a pair of jeans, or use a circle of small hearts on an apron pocket. Group three strawberries together on a shirt front.

Use the patterns on home furnishings, too. They can brighten pillows and curtains, and almost anything else made of fabric. Wouldn't the Little Sun appliqué make a cheerful crib quilt, for instance?

For things to make (as background items for your appliqués), we offer patterns and directions for two bibs. One is a cover-up style for Baby to wear. The other is a burp bib for Mother's shoulder. Also included are directions for making a small handbag; wear it over your shoulder to show off your favorite appliqué.

For each appliqué pattern, there are suggestions for fabric and thread colors (those used on our samples). However, you'll want to select colors that go with the background fabric (shirt or other item) to which the appliqué will be stitched.

For information on preparing and sewing appliqués, you can refer to *General guides for appliqué*, page 2.

To make a baby bib

Fig. 1   Baby Bib
(color photo, page 83)

Materials
½ yd. fabric, 44" wide, for bib fabric and thread for appliqué
(see list of materials for the pattern you choose)
thin polyester batting, 12x18"
thread for stitching and quilting
white self-gripping fastener, ½x1", or large snap

Directions
1. To trace pattern, fold a 13x23" sheet of tracing paper in half down the 23" length. Open, place fold on broken line of Baby Bib pattern, page 92, and trace upper right section. Then trace lower right section, page 93, joining sections on broken lines and adding 2½" to bottom (as noted on pattern).

Refold paper in half. With traced section on the bottom, trace other half of bib. Open and cut out full pattern. Seam allowance of ¼" is included.

2. Cut bib. To cut front, pin pattern to right side of one layer of fabric and cut out. With pencil, mark fold lines A and B in seam allowances.

To cut back, fold bottom of pattern (on line B) out of the way. Pin to one layer of fabric, and cut out. Cut batting to match back.

3. Form crumb pocket on front (Fig. 2), by folding fabric on line A, with wrong side of fabric together. Then fold on line B, with right side of fabric together. (Raw edge of fabric will be even with fold line B.) Press.

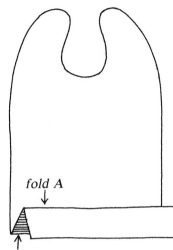

fold A

fold B

Fig. 2 *Folding front to form crumb pocket*

By machine, stitch along edge of fold A (do not catch fold to bib). Baste folds along sides and bottom to hold in place.

4. Prepare and cut appliqué pieces for either hand or machine stitching. (See *General guides for appliqué*, page 2.)

5. Position appliqué pieces on right side of bib front, keeping them at least ½″ from edge of fabric (unless otherwise noted).

Sew in place, and add any embroidery lines. If the appliqué is close to the neck edge, machine-baste on the seam line, ¼″ from the edge; this will be a guide for stitching bib together.

6. Stitch layers together. Stack layers in this order: batting; back, right side up; front, right side down. By machine, stitch layers together with a ¼″

seam; leave 5″ open along one side for turning.

Trim batting close to stitching. Slash fabric seam allowance to stitching along inside neck curve, and cut out small V-shaped pieces on outside curves. Clip across corners. Open seam with iron.

Turn to right side and close opening with hand stitches. Work seam to edge, baste and press lightly.

7. Quilt around bib, ¼″ from edge, and around design. (See *General guides for quilting*, page 5.)

8. Add self-gripping fastener or snap so that one side of neck curve overlaps the other.

To make a burp bib

Fig. 3 Burp Bib *(color photo, page 83)*

Materials
¼ yd. fabric, 44″ wide, for bib fabric and thread for appliqué (see list of materials for the pattern you choose)
thin polyester batting, 9x21″
thread for stitching and quilting

Directions
1. To trace pattern, fold a 9x21″ sheet of tracing paper in half across the 9″ width. Open,

and place fold on broken line of Burp Bib pattern, page 94, and trace.

Refold paper, and cut out both layers to make a full pattern. Seam allowance of ¼″ is included.

2. Cut bib. Fold fabric, right side inside, to make two 9x22″ layers. Pin pattern to fabric and cut. Use the same pattern to cut one layer of batting.

3. Prepare and cut appliqué pieces for either hand or machine stitching. (See *General guides for appliqué*, page 2.)

4. Position appliqué pieces on right side of bib front, keeping them at least 1½″ from all edges. Sew in place, and add any embroidery lines.

5. Stitch layers together. Stack layers in this order: batting; back, right side up; front, right side down. By machine, stitch layers together with a ¼″ seam; leave 4″ open on a straight edge for turning.

Trim batting close to stitching. Slash fabric seam allowance to stitching along inside curves, and cut out small V-shaped pieces on outside curves. Open seam with iron.

Turn to right side and close opening with hand stitches. Work seam to edge, baste and press lightly.

6. Quilt around bib, ¼″ from edge, and around design. (*See General guides for quilting*, page 5.)

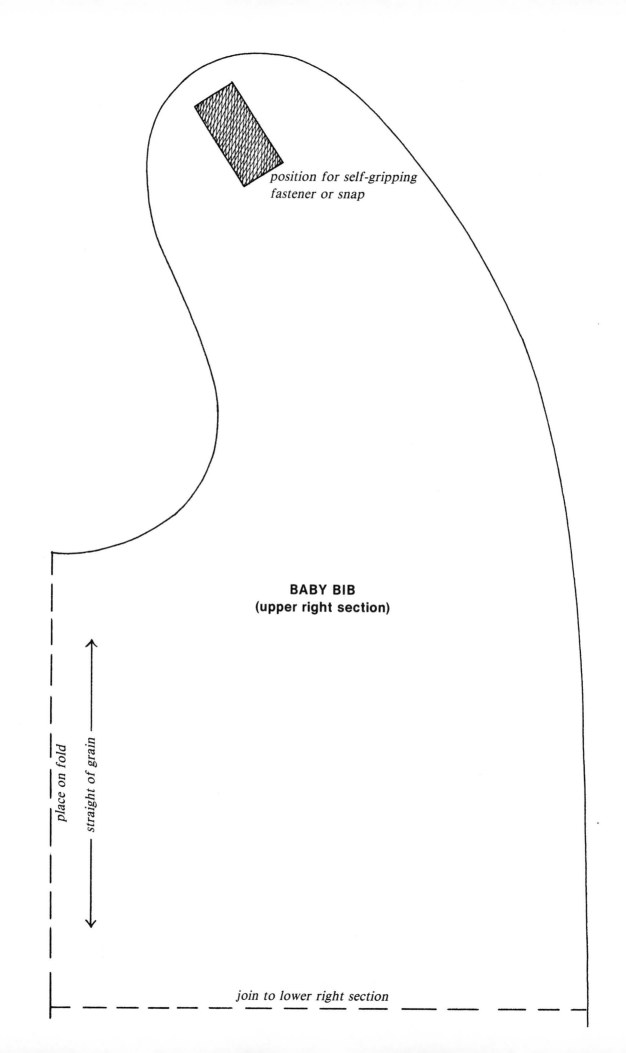

position for self-gripping fastener or snap

BABY BIB
(upper right section)

place on fold

straight of grain

join to lower right section

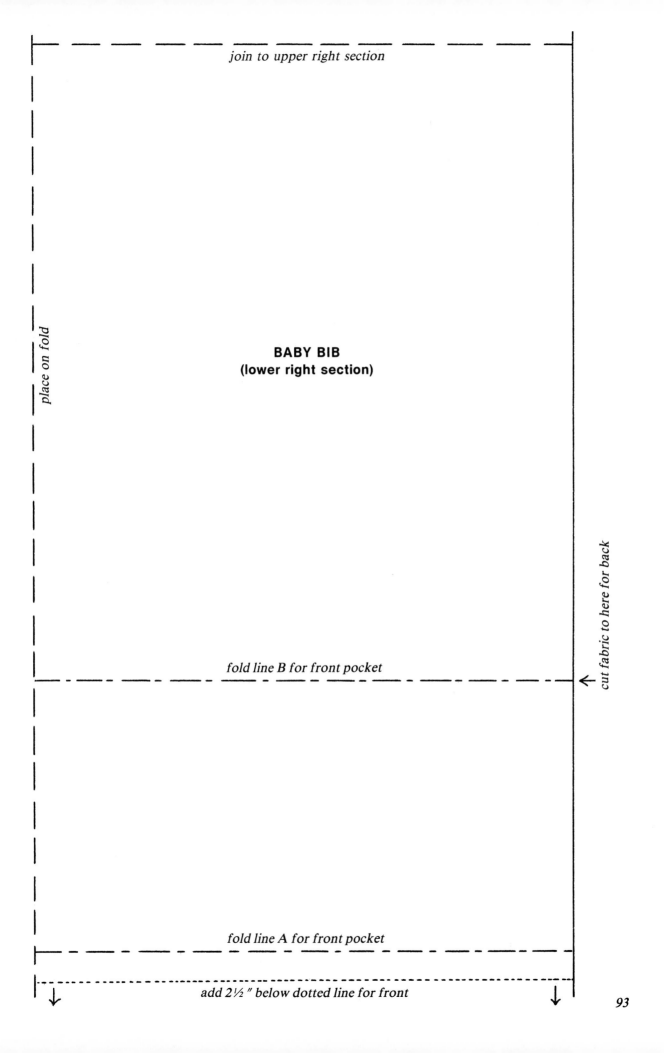

join to upper right section

place on fold

BABY BIB
(lower right section)

cut fabric to here for back

fold line B for front pocket

fold line A for front pocket

add 2½″ below dotted line for front

93

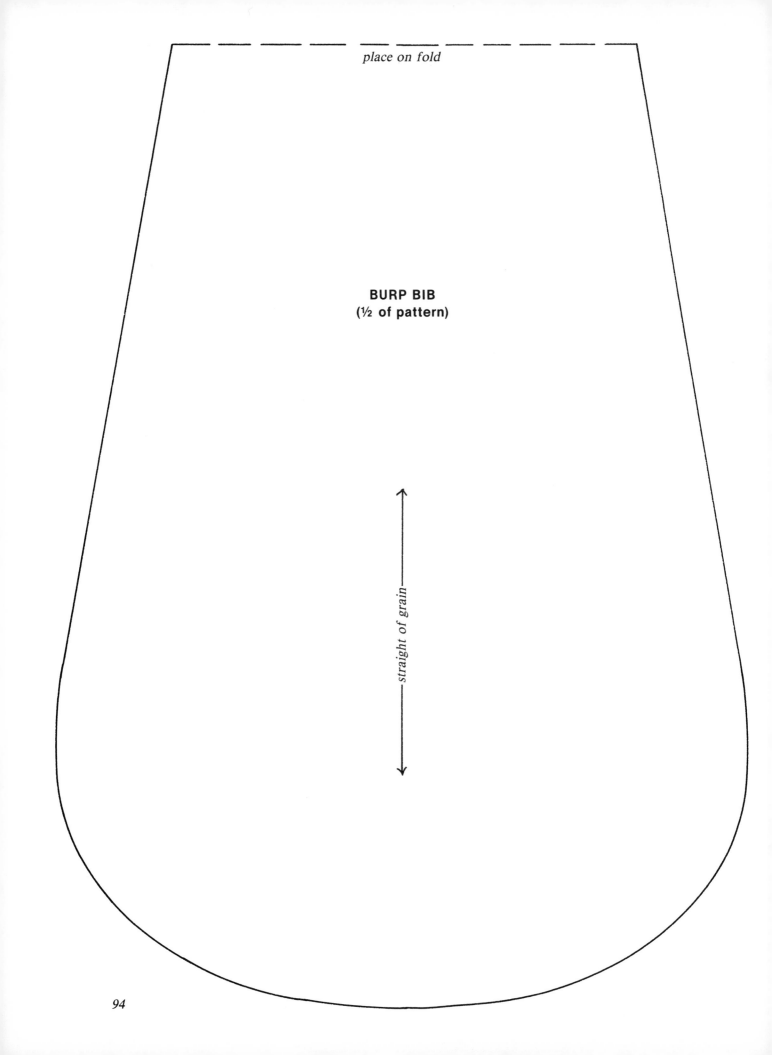

place on fold

BURP BIB
(½ of pattern)

straight of grain

94

To make a shoulder bag

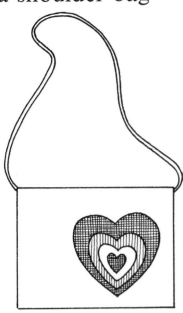

Fig. 4 Shoulder Bag
(color photo, page 83)

Batting gives this bag a soft look. To help bag keep its shape when filled, we added a firm interfacing to the lining.

Materials

firm fabric, 11x16½", for bag
thin polyester batting, 11x16½"
lining fabric, 10x15½"
firm interfacing, 10x14½"
9" zipper to match bag or
   appliqué
18" cord, ¼" diameter, for
   handle, to match bag or
   appliqué
thread for stitching and quilting
fabric and thread for appliqué
   (see list of materials for the
   pattern you choose)

Directions

1. Fold bag fabric in half across the 16½" length, and mark fold with a line of basting; this will be the bottom of the finished bag.

2. Prepare and cut appliqué pieces for either hand or machine stitching. (See *General guides for appliqué,* page 2.)

3. Position appliqué pieces on bag front, keeping them at least 1" from edges and bottom of bag. Sew in place.

4. Layer fabric and batting. Baste batting to wrong side of bag fabric, sewing along edges and across bottom line (Fig. 5).

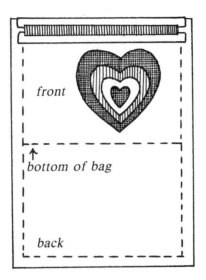

Fig. 5 *Basting layers together; adding zipper at top*

5. Quilt bag around appliqué, if desired. Back appliqué with a piece of muslin (see *General guides for quilting,* page 5).

6. Add zipper. Center zipper along top edge of bag, with right sides together and edges even (Fig. 5). Baste and stitch close to zipper, using zipper foot on machine. Open zipper and restitch closer to the zipper opening.

Fold fabric, right side inside; baste and stitch free edge of zipper tape to opposite edge of bag (Fig. 6). Trim batting close to zipper on both sides. By hand, whip the open ends of zipper tape together (Fig. 7).

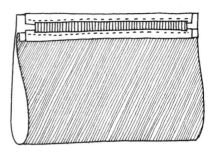

Fig. 6 *Stitching second side of zipper*

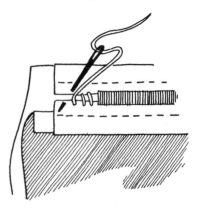

Fig. 7 *Sewing ends of zipper tape together*

7. Close sides. Open zipper a few inches. Pin bag sides together, with zipper teeth at the top.

Position cord inside bag, with each end tight against zipper, and cut ends of cord even with raw edge of fabric. Baste side seams, catching cord and zipper tape. Stitch ½" seams (Fig. 8). Trim batting close to stitching; clip fabric across corners. Turn bag to right side.

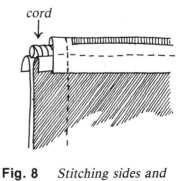

Fig. 8 *Stitching sides and cord*

8. Add lining. Center interfacing on wrong side of lining (½" of lining extends beyond interfacing at each end). Topstitch interfacing to lining along these ends.

Fold layers in half, right side of lining inside. Stitch sides together with ½" seams. Trim interfacing close to stitching. Trim seams to ¼", and clip fabric across corners at bottom.

Fold top edges ½" to wrong side, and press. Tuck lining inside bag, and hand-stitch folded edge of lining to zipper tape.

APPLES

(page 100; color photo, page 14)

Choose between two small apple patterns. For a larger one, see page 53.

Materials
red fabric, 3x3", for small apple
green scrap, for leaf
lightweight, fusible interfacing, 3x4" (for machine appliqué)
thread for stitching
green embroidery floss or thread, for stem and embroidery line

BIRD

(page 100; color photo, page 14)

Use two fabrics. Embroider the wing and eye in a darker color.

Materials
light blue fabric, 4x6", for body and wing (cut as one piece)
peach fabric, 3x4", for breast
lightweight, fusible interfacing, 4x9" (for machine appliqué)
thread for stitching
medium blue embroidery floss or thread, for wing and eye

BLUE RIBBON

(page 100; color photo, page 86)

Cut the blue ribbon in one piece. Appliqué a yellow "1", then embroider ruffle lines in yellow.

Materials
blue fabric, 4x6", for ribbon
yellow scrap, for "1"
lightweight, fusible interfacing, 4x7" (for machine appliqué)
thread for stitching
yellow embroidery floss or thread, for embroidery lines

BOW TIE, COLLAR and BUTTON for bib

(page 101; color photo, page 83)

When cutting collar for either hand or machine stitching, add a ¼" seam allowance to neck edge. This will be caught in the bib seam allowance. You may want to cut three blue fabric "buttons" as we did for our sample bib.

Materials
white fabric, 8x9", for collar
aqua fabric, 3x6", for bow tie (cut as one piece) and three buttons
lightweight, fusible interfacing, 8x12" (for machine appliqué)
white embroidery floss or thread, for embroidery lines on tie

PINK BOW

(page 102; color photo, page 83)

Stitch a pink bow to our cover-up bib, and your favorite little girl will always be dressed up for meals.

Materials
pink fabric, 6x7", for bow

lightweight, fusible interfacing, 6x7" (for machine appliqué)
thread for stitching
medium pink embroidery floss or thread, for embroidery lines

BUTTERFLY

(page 102; color photo, page 83)

We used this pattern on a burp bib, but it would look pretty on a scarf, too.

Materials
green fabric, 5x6", for butterfly
coral scrap, for trim B
yellow scrap, for trim C
lightweight, fusible interfacing, 5x9" (for machine appliqué)
thread for stitching
green embroidery floss or thread, for embroidery lines

CHERRIES

(page 103; color photo, page 14)

Three red cherries can brighten a very small space.

Materials
red scrap, for cherries
green scrap, for leaves
lightweight, fusible interfacing scraps (for machine appliqué)
thread for stitching
green embroidery floss or thread, for stems

CHICK

(page 103; color photo, page 14)

Stitch the wings and legs in yellow. Use black for the eye.

Materials
yellow fabric, 4x4", for chick
lightweight, fusible interfacing, 4x4" (for machine appliqué)

thread for stitching
yellow and black embroidery
   floss or thread, for
   embroidery lines

FOUR-LEAF CLOVER

(page 103; color photo, page 83)

Wish someone (maybe yourself)
good luck with this appliqué.

Materials
green fabric, 6x7", for clover
lightweight, fusible interfacing,
   6x7" (for machine appliqué)
thread for stitching
black embroidery floss or
   thread, for embroidery lines

AQUA DOG

(page 104; color photo, page 14)

Outline the eye pupil in white;
use black for all other embroidery lines.

Materials
aqua fabric, 5x7", for dog (cut
   as one piece)
lightweight, fusible interfacing,
   5x7" (for machine appliqué)
thread for stitching
black and white embroidery
   floss or thread, for
   embroidery lines

DOG WITH BUTTERFLY

(page 104; color photo, page 14)

Choose one color for the dog
and another for the butterfly.
Then reverse colors for embroidery lines.

Materials
bright pink fabric, 4x6", for dog
medium blue fabric, 2½x2½",
   for butterfly

lightweight, fusible interfacing,
   4x8½" (for machine appliqué)
thread for stitching
pink and blue embroidery floss
   or thread, for embroidery
   lines

DUCK

(page 105; color photo, page 14)

This white duck swims in a sea
of blue embroidery stitches.

Materials
white fabric, 5x5", for duck
yellow scrap, for bill
lightweight, fusible interfacing,
   5x6" (for machine appliqué)
thread for stitching
blue embroidery floss or thread,
   for embroidery lines

ELEPHANT

(page 105; color photo, page 86)

This is one white elephant you'll
like to have around. Stitch the
tail and water spray in white;
use a color to match background fabric for eye and ear
embroidery lines.

Materials
white fabric, 5x6", for elephant
lightweight, fusible interfacing,
   5x6" (for machine appliqué)
thread for stitching
white and red embroidery floss
   or thread, for embroidery
   lines

FROG

(page 105; color photo, page 47)

A green frog with yellow eyes
has a big smile for you.

Materials
light green fabric, 5x5", for frog
   (cut as one piece)

dark green fabric, 4x7", for lily
   pad
lightweight, fusible interfacing,
   5x12" (for machine appliqué)
thread for stitching
medium green and gold
   embroidery floss or thread,
   for embroidery lines

STACK OF HEARTS

(page 106; color photo, page 83)

Use one, two, three—or all four
hearts. Stack them as we did on
page 83, using materials below.
Or string several out in a line,
as shown on page 86. You also
could cut seven of one size and
arrange them in a circle.

Materials
deep pink fabric, 7x7", for
   Hearts A and D
light pink fabric, 3x3½", for
   Heart B
medium pink fabric, 5x5", for
   Heart C
lightweight, fusible interfacing,
   8x12" (for machine appliqué)
thread for stitching

HOBBY HORSE

(page 106; color photo, page 47)

Cut the horse from red print,
the rocker and trims from bright
yellow.

Materials
red fabric with yellow print,
   5x6", for horse
yellow-gold fabric, 4x8", for
   mane, tail, saddle and rocker
lightweight, fusible interfacing,
   5x14" (for machine appliqué)
thread for stitching
black embroidery floss or
   thread, for eye and mouth

ICE CREAM CONE

(page 107; color photo, page 47)

Choose a color to match your favorite flavor. Three citrus colors—orange, lemon and lime—make an attractive combination.

Materials

orange and white checked
   fabric, 4x5″, for cone
orange fabric, 5x6″, for ice
   cream
lightweight, fusible interfacing,
   5x10″ (for machine appliqué)
thread for stitching
orange embroidery floss or
   thread, for embroidery lines

LAMB

(page 106; color photo, page 47)

Stitch the legs in white, then embroider the face to match background fabric.

Materials

white fabric, 3½x4″, for lamb
lightweight, fusible interfacing,
   3½x4″ (for machine appliqué)
thread for stitching
white and green embroidery
   floss or thread, for
   embroidery lines

LIGHT BULB

(page 107; color photo, page 47)

The light is "on", with rays embroidered in white.

Materials

white fabric, 4x5″, for bulb
yellow fabric, 2x2″, for base
lightweight, fusible interfacing,
   5x6″ (for machine appliqué)
thread for stitching

black and white embroidery
   floss or thread, for
   embroidery lines

LOLLIPOP FLOWER

(page 107; color photo, page 47)

Pink fabric embroidered with a swirl of deep pink stitches looks good enough to eat. Stitch the stem in green.

Materials

pink fabric, 3½x3½″, for
   flower
green scrap, for leaves
lightweight, fusible interfacing,
   4x5″ (for machine appliqué)
thread for stitching
deep pink and green embroidery
   floss or thread, for
   embroidery lines

MINNOW

(page 108; color photo, page 86)

Use this little fish alone, or appliqué a whole school of colorful minnows.

Materials

yellow fabric, 3x4″, for one fish
lightweight, fusible interfacing,
   3x4″ (for machine appliqué)
thread for stitching
turquoise embroidery floss or
   thread, for embroidery lines

PARROT

(page 108; color photo, page 47)

Four solid colors make up this bright jungle bird.

Materials

bright green fabric, 4x7″, for
   body

turquoise fabric, 2½x4″, for
   wing
red fabric, 2½x2½″, for top of
   wing
yellow-gold scrap, for beak, eye
   and claw
lightweight, fusible interfacing,
   7x9″ (for machine appliqué)
thread for stitching
black embroidery floss or
   thread, for embroidery lines

PENGUIN

(page 108; color photo, page 50)

Stitch along the top edge of each wing (neck to wing tip) in blue; appliqué rest of design with matching thread. Embroider a white eye and mouth, and add a blue line to separate wings from body.

Materials

white fabric, 4½x5½″, for body
medium blue fabric, 3½x4″, for
   head and feet
lightweight, fusible interfacing,
   4½x9″ (for machine appliqué)
thread for stitching
blue and white embroidery floss
   or thread, for embroidery
   lines

POLAR BEAR

(page 108; color photo, page 50)

You may want to outline the bear with the same color floss or thread used for inside design lines.

Materials

white fabric, 5x6″, for bear (cut
   as one piece)
lightweight, fusible interfacing,
   5x6″ (for machine appliqué)
thread for stitching
blue embroidery floss or thread,
   for embroidery lines

FLAT ROSE

(page 109; color photo, page 86)

Cut rose in one piece, then embroider petal lines. For stem, trim double-fold bias to make a narrow single-fold bias. Attach stem by hand or with a machine zigzag stitch (set for medium length and narrow width—not a satin stitch).

Materials

bright pink fabric, 5½x5½", for rose
green fabric, 4x4½", for leaves
green double-fold bias binding, ¼" wide, in length desired for stem
lightweight, fusible interfacing, 5½x9½" (for machine appliqué)
thread for stitching
rose embroidery floss or thread, for embroidery lines

SNAIL

(page 109; color photo, page 50)

We used a solid color for the body and a blending polka dot print for the shell. Embroidery lines are in a deeper shade.

Materials

lavender fabric, 3x5", for body
lavender fabric with white dots, 3½x4", for shell
lightweight, fusible interfacing, 3½x9" (for machine appliqué)
thread for stitching
purple embroidery floss or thread, for embroidery lines

SNAKE

(page 110; color photo, page 50)

This friendly snake is tied up in a knot. Embroider the tongue in red; use green for all other lines.

Materials

light green fabric, 9x11", for snake
lightweight, fusible interfacing, 9x11" (for machine appliqué)
thread for stitching
red and dark green embroidery floss or thread, for embroidery lines

STRAWBERRY

(page 110; color photo, page 86)

Red fabric with white polka dots is perfect for this design. Appliqué a single berry—or use half a dozen to form a ring.

Materials

red fabric with white dots, 2½x2½", for one strawberry
green scrap, for leaf
lightweight, fusible interfacing, 2½x3½" (for machine appliqué)
thread for stitching
green embroidery floss or thread, for stem

LITTLE SUN

(page 111; color photo, page 50)

Add a bright note to a jacket, vest or wall hanging with this happy face. Embroider eye pupils in black, and all other lines in orange.

Materials

orange fabric, 9x9", for sun
yellow-gold fabric, 5x5", for face
lightweight, fusible interfacing, 9x14" (for machine appliqué)
thread for stitching
orange and black embroidery floss or thread, for face design

TURTLE

(page 112; color photo, page 50)

Cut the design in one piece, then embroider lines in blue.

Materials

red fabric with white dots, 4½x7", for turtle
lightweight, fusible interfacing, 4½x7" (for machine appliqué)
thread for stitching
blue embroidery floss or thread, for embroidery lines

UMBRELLA GIRL

(page 112; color photo, page 50)

Combine two fabrics, then add embroidery details in black.

Materials

orange fabric, 3x3½", for body
green fabric, 3x6", for umbrella and boots
lightweight, fusible interfacing, 3x9½" (for machine appliqué)
thread for stitching
black embroidery floss or thread, for embroidery lines

WHALE

(page 112; color photo, page 86)

Blue stitches form ocean waves under this smiling whale.

Materials

orange fabric, 3½x5", for whale
lightweight, fusible interfacing, 3½x5" (for machine appliqué)
thread for stitching
blue embroidery floss or thread, for embroidery lines

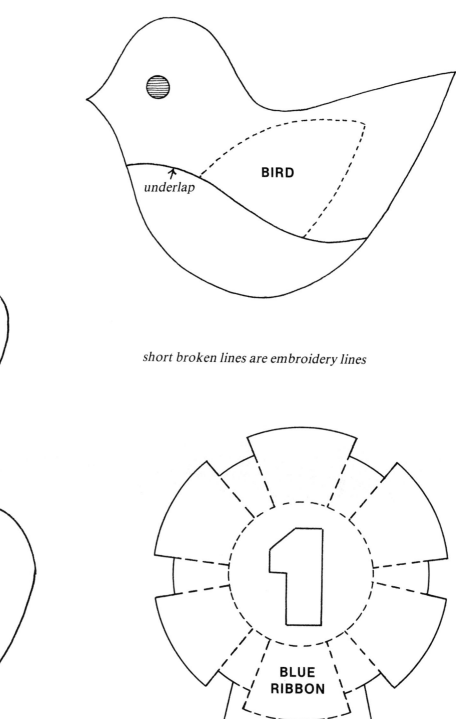

BIRD

underlap

short broken lines are embroidery lines

APPLE

APPLE

1

BLUE RIBBON

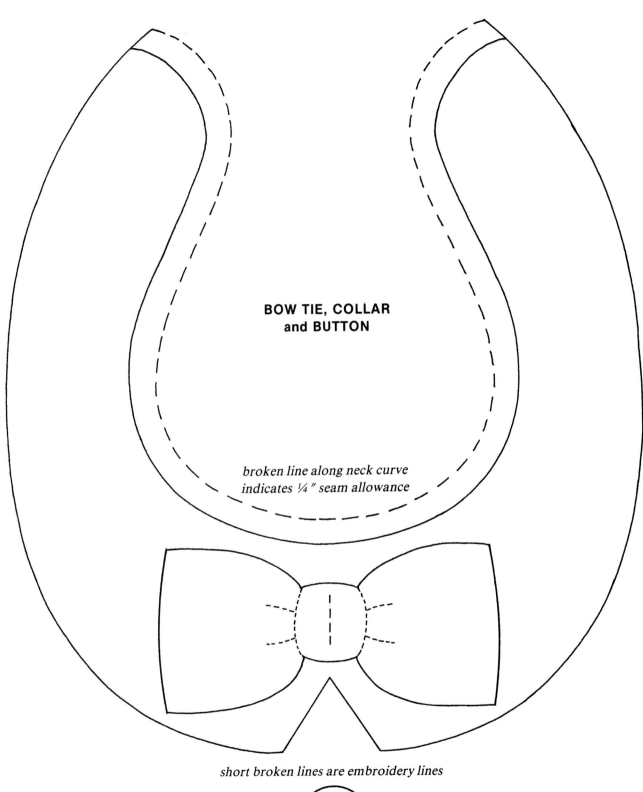

**BOW TIE, COLLAR
and BUTTON**

*broken line along neck curve
indicates ¼″ seam allowance*

short broken lines are embroidery lines

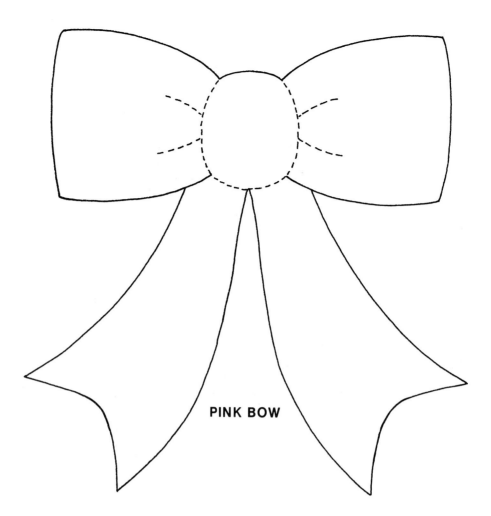

PINK BOW

short broken lines are embroidery lines

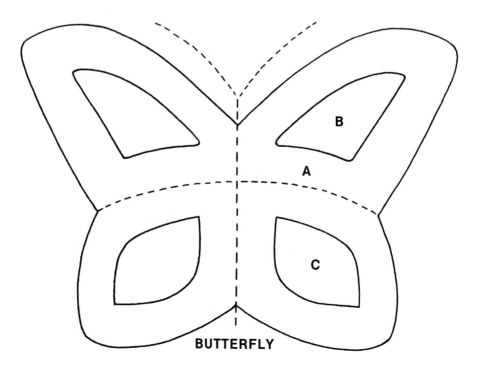

BUTTERFLY

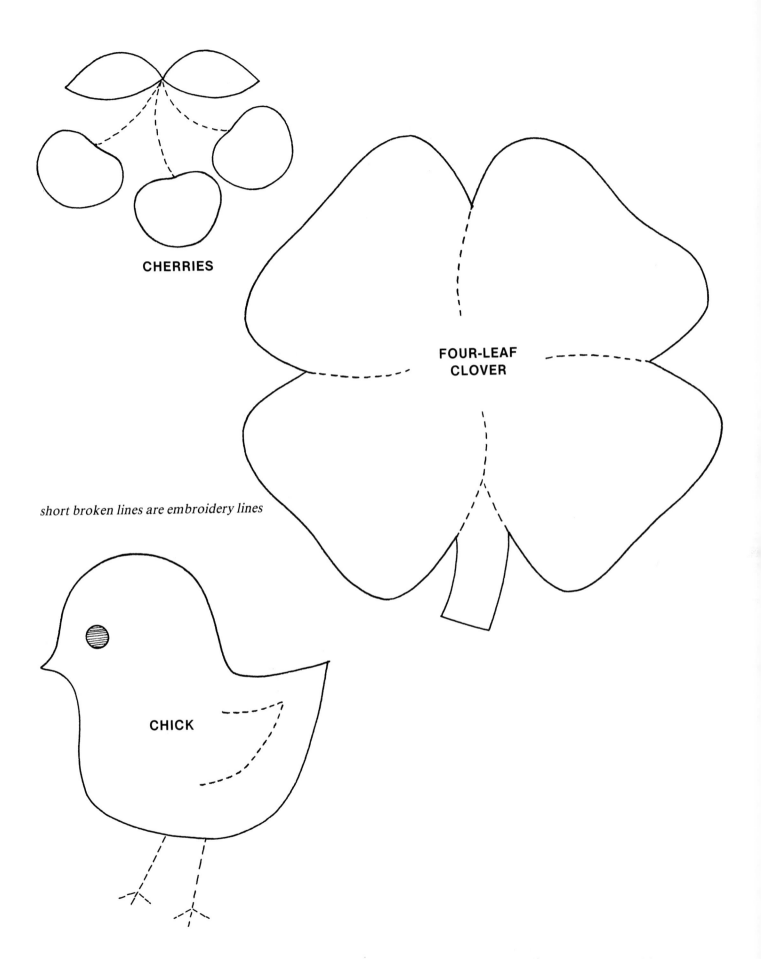

CHERRIES

FOUR-LEAF CLOVER

short broken lines are embroidery lines

CHICK

DOG WITH BUTTERFLY

short broken lines are embroidery lines

AQUA DOG

ELEPHANT

short broken lines are embroidery lines

DUCK

FROG

underlap

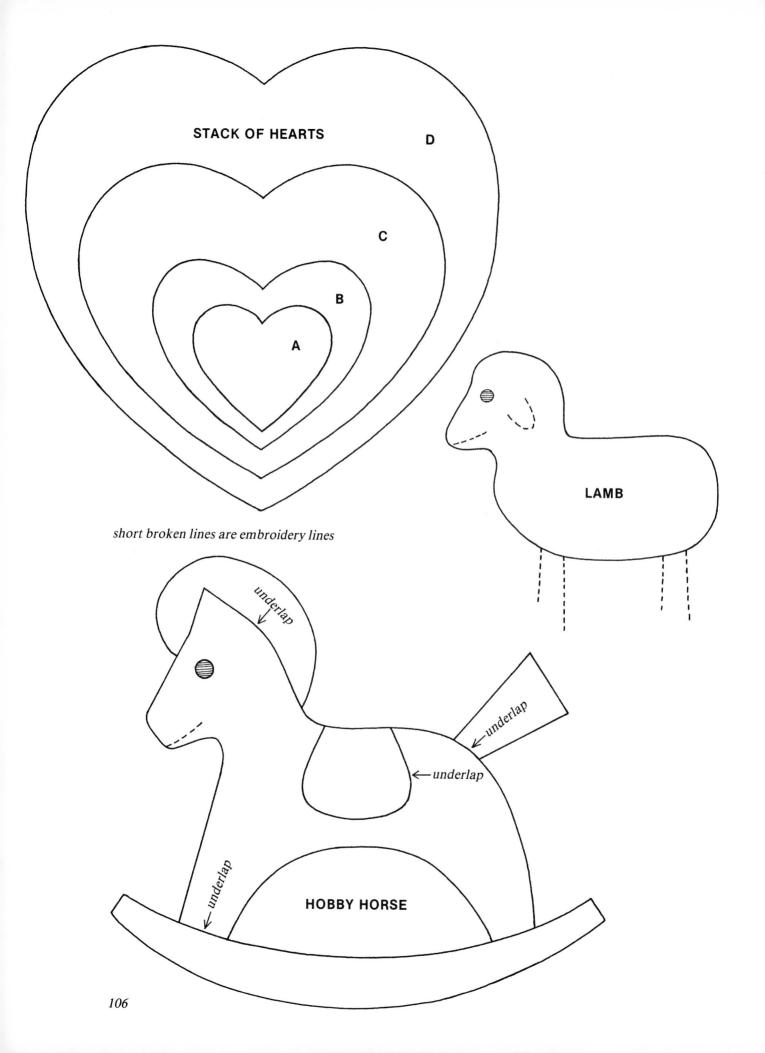

STACK OF HEARTS

D

C

B

A

short broken lines are embroidery lines

LAMB

underlap

underlap

underlap

underlap

HOBBY HORSE

106

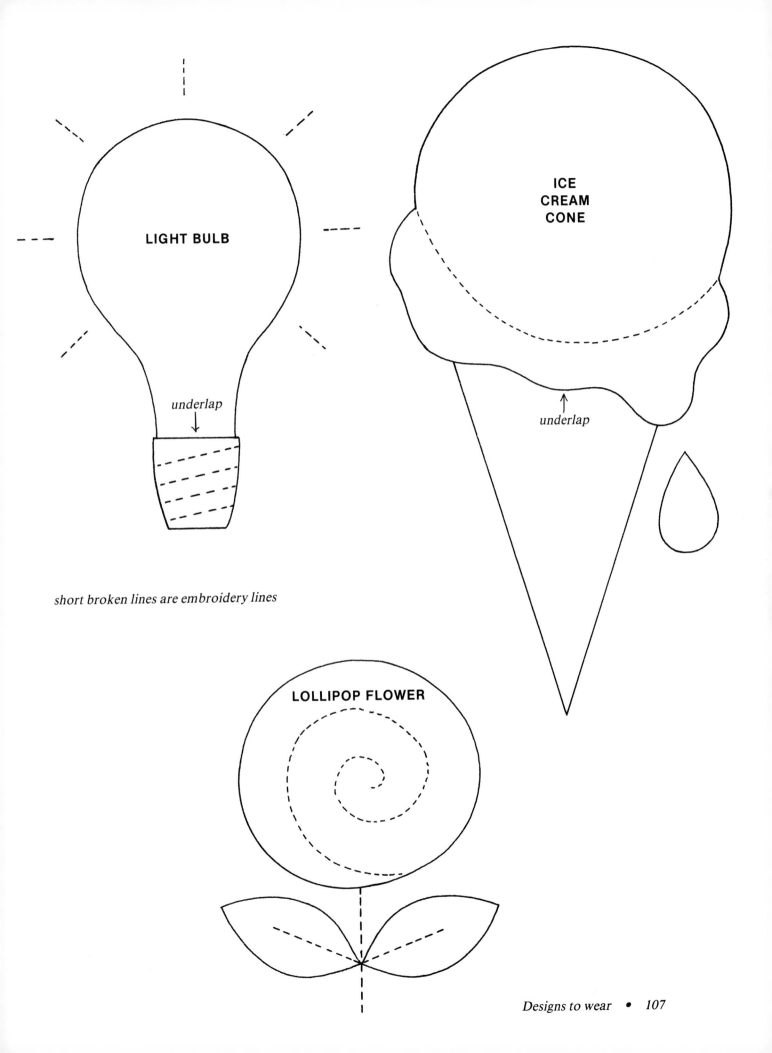

LIGHT BULB

underlap

short broken lines are embroidery lines

ICE CREAM CONE

underlap

LOLLIPOP FLOWER

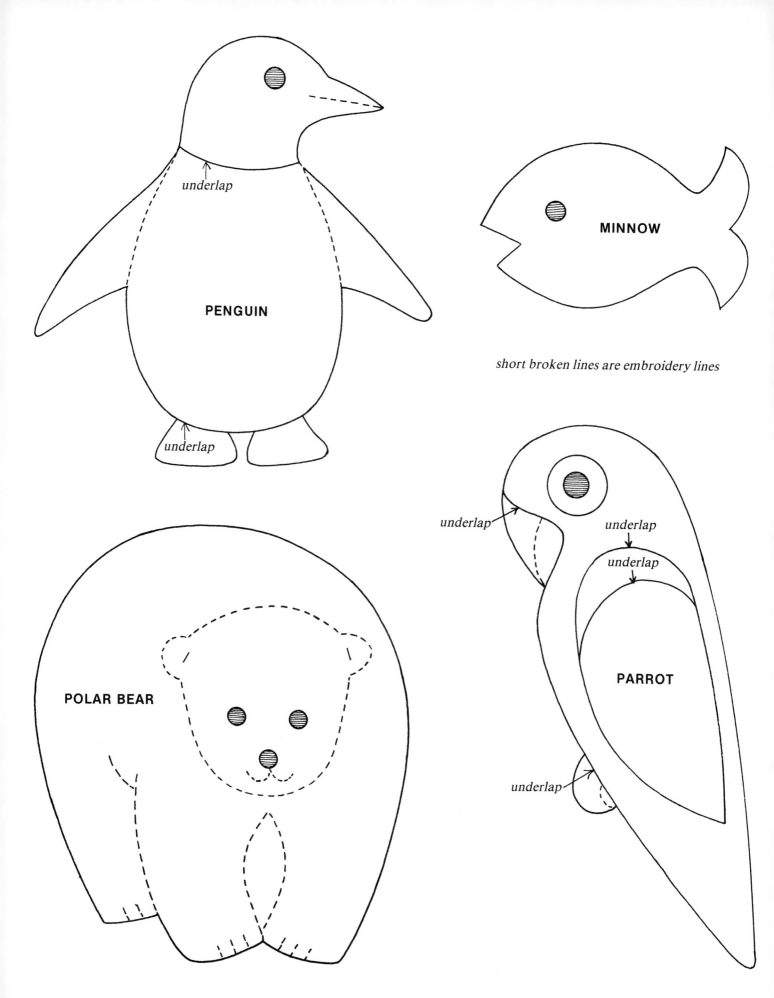

PENGUIN

underlap

underlap

MINNOW

short broken lines are embroidery lines

POLAR BEAR

PARROT

underlap

underlap

underlap

underlap

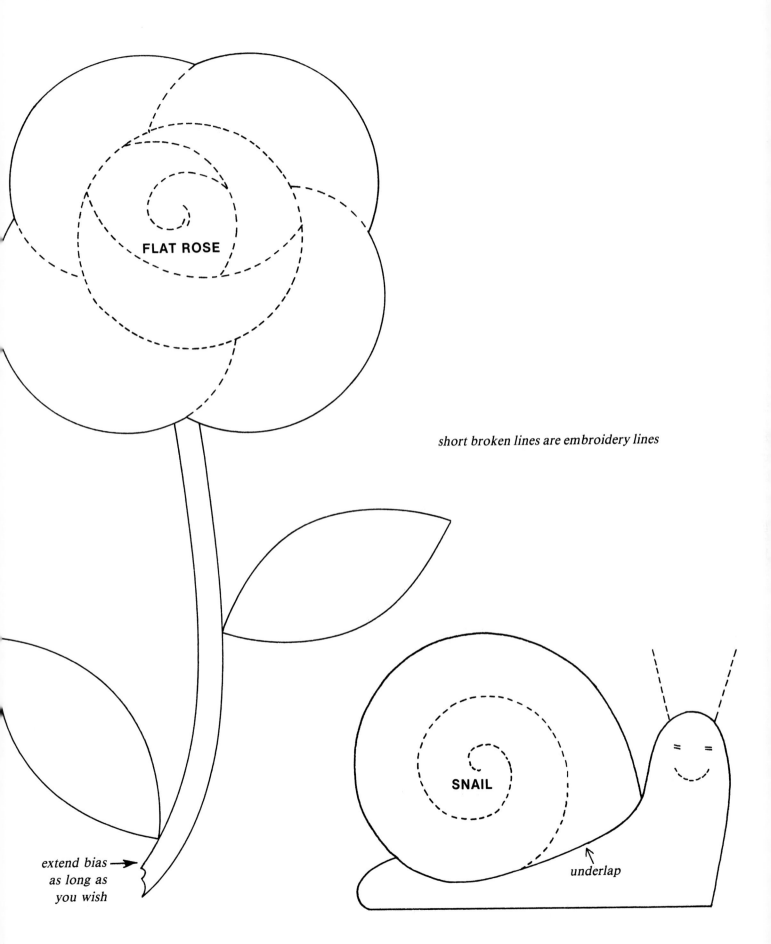

FLAT ROSE

short broken lines are embroidery lines

extend bias →
as long as
you wish

SNAIL

underlap

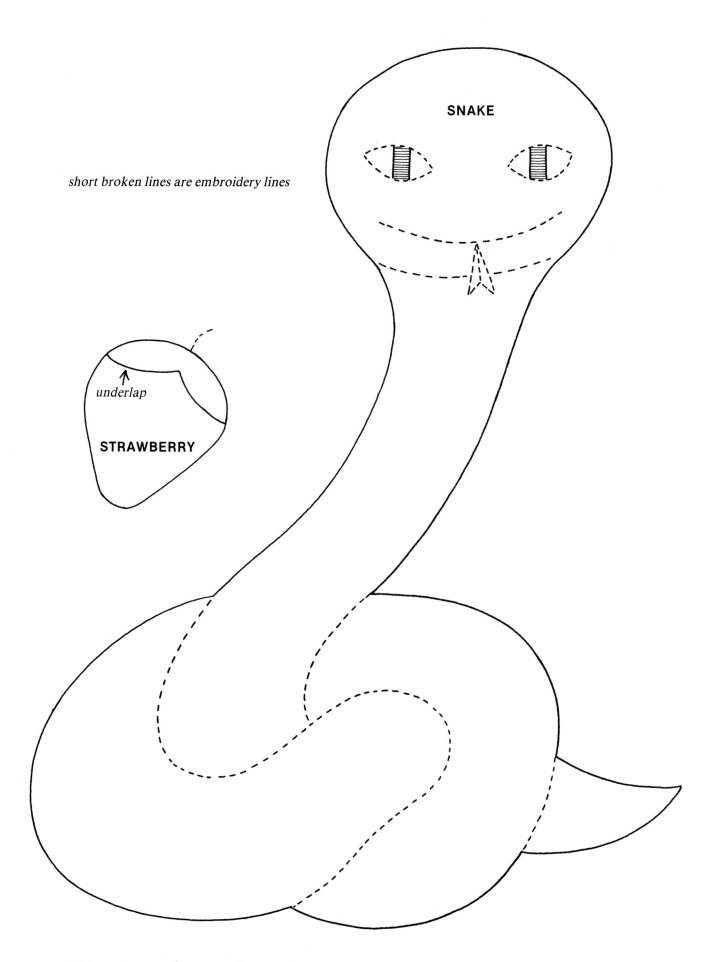

short broken lines are embroidery lines

SNAKE

underlap

STRAWBERRY

LITTLE SUN

underlap

short broken lines are embroidery lines

TURTLE

short broken lines are embroidery lines

UMBRELLA GIRL

underlap

↑
underlap

WHALE

8

Stuffed Ornaments

Fabric ornaments can brighten your home in many ways, and their softness adds a warm, cozy touch to any room.

Small stuffed ornaments make wonderful trimmings for a Christmas tree because they won't break. So we've included six miniatures that are just the right size, each about 4″ wide.

There are also patterns for a trio of acrobatic clowns stitched in holiday colors. They can add fun to your Christmas tree or be hung on the wall for year-round enjoyment.

Two slightly larger patterns, one for a shell and one for a pieced work design called Repeat X, can be used as pincushions to display—and to use.

For a dramatic decorative accessory, make a soft sculpture in the shape of a fish or a sun. Each one is stitched and stuffed, then mounted on a wooden dowel. Picture a school of three fish floating over the top of a bookcase. Or stand the Little Sun on a window sill—its good-natured smile will radiate sunshine even on cloudy days.

To make other stuffed ornaments, choose from the appliqué patterns found in Chapters 2-7. You can even turn some of these patterns into soft toys (they travel more comfortably than noisy ones).

To make a stuffed ornament

1. Complete front of ornament, following directions for the pattern you choose.

2. Stitch front to back, right sides together, by hand or machine; leave opening for turning.

3. Trim seams. Slash fabric to stitching on any V areas or inside curves. Clip out small V-shaped pieces on outside curves; clip across corners. If batting is used, trim to stitching. Open seam with iron.

4. Turn to right side, work seam to edge and press lightly. Stuff loosely with fiberfill, keeping ornament flat to show design. Close seam with hand stitches.

5. Complete ornament in one of the following ways.

For a pincushion or soft toy, close opening with hand stitches.

For a hanging ornament, close opening with hand stitches. Add ribbon or cord (make loop if desired).

For a free-standing sculpture on a dowel, push one end of dowel about 2½″ into ornament through bottom opening. Arrange fiberfill so ornament is smooth. Remove dowel, spread glue on the 2½″ section, reinsert in ornament and press against stuffing. Wipe off excess glue. Close opening around dowel with hand stitches (not necessary on Little Sun).

In center of wooden base, drill a hole ¼″ in diameter and 1″ deep. Sand top and sides smooth, then insert free end of dowel in hole.

DIAMOND STAR (miniature)

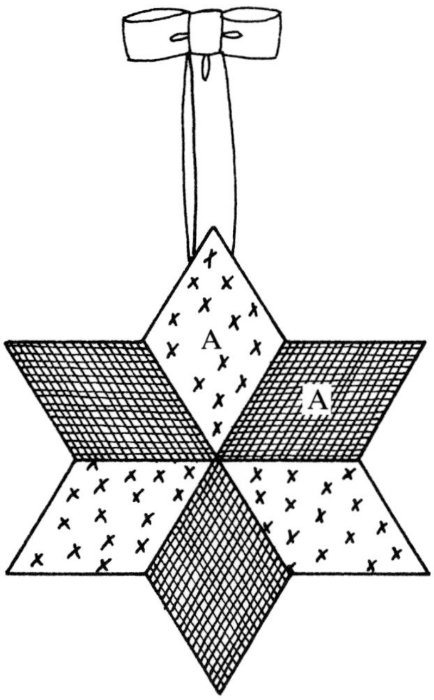

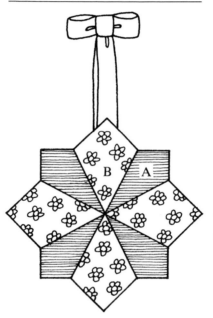

Fig. 1   Diamond Star
(color photo, page 119)

One pattern piece and two fabrics form this design. The back of the ornament is plain.

Materials

red fabric, 6x8", for design and
*   back*
red print, 4x6", for design
polyester fiberfill
thread for stitching
ribbon, ¼" wide, for hanging

Directions

See *General guides for pieced work*, page 5.
1. Trace pattern for Diamond Star A and Back, page 124. Make a template for each piece.
2. Place templates on *wrong* side of fabric. On red, trace three A pieces and one Back. On print, trace three A pieces. Cut out fabric, adding a ¼" seam allowance.
3. Lay pieces flat, right side up, to form design in Fig. 1. By hand, join two diamonds, stitch-

ing from outside edge to end of seam (pencil) line; do not stitch into seam allowance. Add one more diamond to complete half of star.

Join remaining diamonds to complete other half, then join the two halves.
4. Stitch front to back, stuff and finish; see *To make a stuffed ornament*, page 113.

HOME AGAIN (miniature)

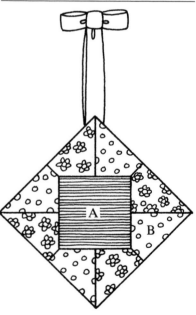

Fig. 2   Home Again
(color photo, page 119)

The front of this ornament uses the center portion of a traditional quilt block design. The back is cut in one piece.

Materials

red fabric, 5x9", for design and
*   back*
green print, 5x6", for design
polyester fiberfill
thread for stitching
ribbon, ¼" wide, for hanging

Directions

See *General guides for pieced work*, page 5.

1. Trace pattern pieces A, B and Back for Home Again, page 124. Make a template for each piece.
2. Place templates on *wrong* side of fabric. On red, trace four A pieces and one Back. On green print, trace four B pieces. Cut out fabric, adding a ¼" seam allowance.
3. Lay pieces flat, right side up, to form design in Fig. 2. By hand, join an A to a B, stitching from outside edge to end of seam (pencil) line; do not stitch into seam allowance.

Join another A and B, then stitch the two sections together to form half the design.

Repeat to make other half. Join the two halves to complete the design.
4. Stitch front to back, stuff and finish; see *To make a stuffed ornament*, page 113.

SQUARE PEG (miniature)

Fig. 3   Square Peg
(color photo, page 119)

For this ornament, we took the center portion of another traditional quilt block design. Add a little embroidery to the center square, if you like.

Materials

green fabric, 5x7", for design and back
red print, 4x5", for design
green and white print, 4x5", for design
polyester fiberfill
thread for stitching
ribbon, ¼" wide, for hanging

Directions

See *General guides for pieced work*, page 5.
1. Trace pattern pieces A, B and Back for Square Peg, page 125. Make a template for each piece.
2. Place templates on *wrong* side of fabric. On green, trace one A and one Back. On red print, trace four B pieces. On green and white print, trace four B-reversed pieces. Cut out, adding a ¼" seam allowance.
3. Lay pieces flat, right side up, to form design in Fig. 3.
    Make the four corners by joining each green and white print B to a red print B, stitching from raw edge to raw edge.
    Join each corner section to green square A, sewing only on seam (pencil) lines; do not stitch into seam allowances. Then join B pieces at each corner of A.
4. Stitch front to back, stuff and finish; see *To make a stuffed ornament*, page 113.

BIRD (miniature)

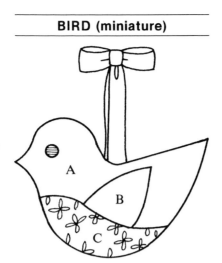

Fig. 4   Bird
(color photo, page 119)

This ornament has a design on both sides. Make the wings from separate pieces of fabric and stitch them onto the body, rather than outlining them with embroidery.

Materials

red fabric, 7x8", for body and wings
red print, 4x5", for breast
polyester fiberfill
thread for stitching
black embroidery floss or thread, for eye
ribbon, ¼" wide, for hanging

Directions

See *General guides for pieced work*, page 5.
1. Trace pattern for Bird, page 100. Make a template for each piece, A-C (see Fig. 4).
2. Place templates on *wrong* side of fabric. On red, trace one A, one A-reversed, two B and two B-reversed pieces. On red print, trace one C and one C-reversed piece.
3. Lay pieces flat, right side up, to form two designs as in Fig. 4 (one bird will be reversed). Clip seam allowance on inside curves

almost to seam line. By hand, join each A to each C.
4. Satin-stitch eyes in black.
5. To make each wing, sew a B to a B-reversed, right sides together; leave opening at bottom for turning. Trim seams, turn to right side, stuff lightly and close opening by hand. After bird is stuffed, sew a wing to each side of body, leaving top of wing free.
6. Stitch front to back, stuff and finish bird; see *To make a stuffed ornament*, page 113.

HEART (miniature)

Fig. 5   Heart
(color photo, page 119)

Two appliquéd hearts repeat the shape of this ornament.

Materials

red print fabric, 6x10", for front, back and design
green fabric, 3x4", for design
lightweight, fusible interfacing, 3x7" (for machine appliqué)
polyester fiberfill
thread for stitching
ribbon, ¼" wide, for hanging

Directions

See *General guides for appliqué*, page 2.

1. Trace pattern for Stack of Hearts, page 106, omitting large heart D. Make a template for each piece, A-C.
2. On *wrong* side of red print, trace two C pieces for front and back. Cut out, adding a ¼" seam allowance. On one piece, baste around edge directly over seam line (this will be the front).
3. Prepare and cut appliqué pieces for either hand or machine stitching. Use red print for one A piece and green for one B piece.
4. Position appliqué pieces on right side of front, and sew in place.
5. Stitch front to back, stuff and finish heart; see *To make a stuffed ornament*, page 113.

BUTTERFLY (miniature)

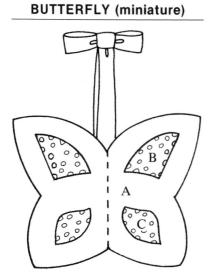

Fig. 6   Butterfly
(color photo, page 119)

Decorate the wings with appliqués, and quilt a line up the center.

Materials
green fabric, 6x10", for body
green and white print, 4x4½",
    for trim
lightweight, fusible interfacing,
    4x4½" (for machine appliqué)

polyester fiberfill
thread for stitching and quilting
ribbon, ¼" wide, for hanging

Directions
See *General guides for appliqué*, page 2.
1. Trace pattern for Butterfly, page 102. Make a template for each piece, A-C.
2. On *wrong* side of green fabric, trace two A pieces for front and back. Cut out, adding a ¼" seam allowance. On one piece, baste around edge directly over seam line (this will be the front).
3. Prepare and cut appliqué pieces for either hand or machine stitching. Use print for one B, one B-reversed, one C and one C-reversed piece.
4. Position appliqué pieces on right side of front, and sew in place.
5. Stitch front to back, stuff and finish butterfly; see *To make a stuffed ornament*, page 113. Quilt a line up the center before adding ribbon for hanging.

ACROBATIC CLOWNS

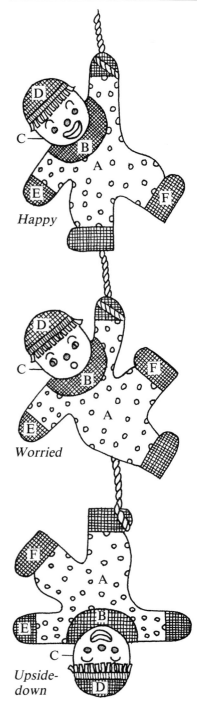

Happy

Worried

Upside-down

Fig. 7   Acrobatic Clowns
(color photo, page 119)

All three clown patterns could be flat appliqués. To turn them into 6"-high ornaments or soft toys, we appliquéd face and trims to one side of each complete clown shape, then added a plain back. The neck ruffle can be a flat appliqué or a gathered strip of fabric.

Materials (for one clown)

2 pieces red (or green) fabric
with white dots, 8x8″ each,
for front and back
green (or red) fabric to contrast
with clown, 6x6″, for trim
white fabric, 3x3″, for face
polyester fiberfill
thread for stitching and quilting
red, blue and black embroidery
floss or thread, for face
4″ narrow red fringe, for trim
cord, ¼″ diameter, for hanging

Directions

See *General guides for appliqué,* page 2.
1. Trace pattern for clown, page 126, 127 or 128. Make a template for the complete clown and for each piece, A-F. Label all templates. (Keep pieces for each clown separate.)
2. On *right* side of one piece of dotted fabric, trace template for complete clown. Then use templates A-F to mark positions for appliqués. Do not cut fabric.
3. Prepare and cut appliqué pieces for hand stitching. Use white for one C, and transfer design lines for face.

Use contrasting color for one D, two E and two F pieces (reverse one F for Happy and Upside-down Clowns).

Cut one flat ruffle (B), or a 2x6″ strip for gathered ruffle. (To make gathered ruffle, fold strip lengthwise, right side out, and stitch a gathering line ¼″ from raw edge. Ruffle will be gathered to fit under face; raw ends will be caught in outside seam.)
4. Position appliqué pieces on right side of clown and baste in place. To layer pieces on head, add ruffle (flat or gathered), then face, then hat.

Turn and hand-stitch raw edges that run across inside of clown. Leave all outside edges flat, to be caught in the seam when front is stitched to back.
5. Embroider face, using red for mouth and nose, blue for eyes, and black for eyebrows. Use black to outline eyes on Worried Clown.
6. Baste around clown directly over seam (pencil) line to transfer seam line to wrong side.

Pin clown front to back fabric, right sides together. Machine-stitch directly over basted seam line, leaving an opening on a straight edge for turning.

Cut around clown, leaving ¼″ for seam allowance. Slash seam allowance to stitching in V areas and along inside curves. Clip out V-shaped pieces in outside curves; clip across corners. Open seam with iron.

Turn to right side, work seam to edge and press lightly. Stuff loosely, keeping clown flat. Close opening with hand stitches. By hand, quilt a line along bottom edge of face. Add fringe to edge of hat, fringe side toward face. Sew cord to one mitt (or foot) for hanging.

REPEAT X (pincushion)

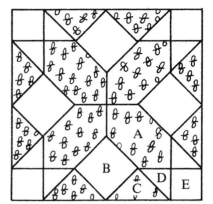

Fig. 8   Repeat X
(color photo, page 122)

Here's a challenge to stitch by hand. To add some pieces, you must pivot at a point, doing the stitching in two steps.

This pieced design is 6″ square. To make a 14″-square pillow top, you could stitch four small blocks together, then add a 1″ border.

Materials

print fabric, 8x16″, for design
and back
orange fabric, 8x9″, for design
polyester batting and muslin,
6½x6½″ each, for quilting
polyester fiberfill
thread for stitching and quilting

Directions

See *General guides for pieced work,* page 5.
1. Trace pattern pieces A-E and Back for Repeat X, page 125. Make a template for each piece.
2. Place templates on *wrong* side of fabric. On print, trace one Back, four A and eight C pieces. On orange, trace four B, eight D and four E pieces. Cut out, adding a ¼″ seam allowance.
3. Lay pieces flat, right side up, to form design in Fig. 8, and hand-stitch pieces together.

Begin by forming diagonal units. Join one orange D to an orange E; join a second orange D to a print A. Then stitch each D-E unit to an A-D unit.

Join the diagonal units in pairs by stitching two A pieces together. Sew from raw edge at center of block design and end stitching on seam (pencil) line at other edge (where a B will be added). Join the pairs of diagonal units to form center of block, stitching only on the seam line; do not stitch into seam allowances.

Complete four large triangles by stitching two print C pieces to each orange B. Then join each large triangle to the center section, keeping stitches at the pivot point on the seam lines.
4. Place completed block, right side up, over layers of batting and muslin, and quilt. (See *General guides for quilting*, page 5.) Finish by basting layers together around edge on seam line.
5. Stitch front to back, stuff and finish; see *To make a stuffed ornament*, page 113.

SHELL (pincushion)

Fig. 9 Shell
(color photo, page 122)

Here's a new appliqué pattern, but many of the designs in Chapter 7 would fit on this 6"-square pincushion.

Materials

*2 pieces green print, 6½x6½"
    each, for front and back
yellow fabric, 5x6", for shell
polyester batting and muslin,
    6½x6½" each, for quilting
    (optional)
polyester fiberfill
thread for stitching and quilting
medium green embroidery floss
    or thread, for embroidery
    lines*

Directions

See *General guides for appliqué*, page 2.
1. Trace pattern for Shell, page 129, and make a template.
2. Use yellow fabric to prepare and cut appliqué for either hand or machine stitching.
3. Position appliqué on right side of pincushion front (green print square), and sew in place.
4. Add embroidery lines in medium green.
5. To quilt (optional), place appliquéd square, right side up, over layers of batting and muslin. (See *General guides for quilting*, page 5.)
6. Stitch front to back, stuff and finish; see *To make a stuffed ornament*, page 113.

FISH (on dowel)

Fig. 10 Fish
(color photo, page 122)

Mount three fish on dowels of different lengths, and use them together as a decorating accessory. You can appliqué the eye, as we did, or embroider it in a satin stitch.

Materials (for one fish, with appliqué on one side)

*2 pieces green, blue or turquoise
    fabric, 7x9" each, for front
    and back
scrap of contrasting color, for
    eye
scrap of lightweight, fusible
    interfacing (for machine
    appliqué)
2 layers thin polyester batting,
    7x9" each
polyester fiberfill
thread for stitching
regular or quilting thread in
    contrasting color, for quilting
10"-long dowel, ¼" diameter
    (For three fish, cut dowels
    10", 12" and 14" long.)
4" length of 2x3" lumber, for
    base
white glue*

(continued on page 123)

Stitch some miniatures, using appliqué and pieced work, for holiday decorating. Left to right, the designs are Diamond Star (page 114), Heart (page 115), Square Peg (page 114), Butterfly (page 116), Bird (page 115) and Home Again (page 114).

Hang these three Acrobatic Clowns from a Christmas tree or a dowel. Left to right, they are named Happy, Upside-down and Worried, and directions for making them are on page 116.

120

Carry an eye-catching tote, with an appliqué or pieced work design on the front. On the opposite page, top row and left to right, the designs are Bouquet (page 31) and Peeping Cat (page 30). Below is the Big Sun (page 30), shown as an appliqué on a tote and as a quilted design on a pillow top. On this page, top row and left to right, are Signs of Spring (page 33) and Folded Rose (page 31). Below is Will-o'-the-Wisp (page 32).

Stuff a few ornaments, like
the Little Sun (page 123) and
the Fish (page 118), and
mount them on wooden
dowels. For pincushions, try
the Shell at left (page 118) or
the Repeat X (page 117).

122

(continued from page 118)

Directions

See *General guides for appliqué*, page 2.

1. Trace pattern for Fish in the Sea (fish only), page 79. For gill curve by eye, copy bottom half of line only; omit top half of curve (see Fig. 10). Make templates for fish and eye.

2. On *right* side of one 7x9″ piece of fabric, place template for fish, right side up. Trace outline and transfer design lines. (This will be the front.) Do not cut fabric.

3. Use contrasting fabric to prepare and cut one eye appliqué for either hand or machine stitching.

4. Position eye on right side of fish front and sew in place.

5. Baste around fish directly over outside seam (pencil) line to transfer seam line to wrong side. Mark point where bottom fin begins (see dot on Fig. 10); you will begin stitching here when joining front to back.

Pin fish front to back fabric, right sides together. Machine-stitch directly over basted seam line, beginning at fin mark; leave opening along bottom for turning. Remove basting.

6. Add batting. Place fish, front side down, over two layers of batting. Machine-stitch directly over seam line, leaving the opening for turning.

Trim batting to seam line. Cut out fabric around fish, leaving just under ¼″ for seam allowance. Clip into V areas and inside curves.

7. Turn to right side, work seam to edge and press lightly. Partially close opening by hand, stitching from gill curve toward mouth.

Stitch (quilt) design lines by hand or machine, using thread to match eye. Stuff lightly with fiberfill, keeping fish flat and smooth.

8. Insert dowel and finish fish; see *To make a stuffed ornament*, Step 5, page 113.

LITTLE SUN (on dowel)

Fig. 11 Little Sun
(color photo, page 122)

Two sun shapes, each made double, are stitched together so rays on the back unit "shine" through rays on the front.

Materials

*4 squares orange fabric, 9x9″
   each, for sun
2 squares thin polyester batting,
   9x9″ each
polyester fiberfill
thread for stitching
yellow-gold and black embroidery floss or thread, for face
12″ dowel, ¼″ diameter
4″ length of 2x3″ lumber, for
   base
white glue*

Directions

See *General guides for appliqué*, page 2, for making template.

1. Trace pattern for Little Sun, page 111, and make one template (sun will be cut in one piece).

2. On *right* side of one orange square, place template, right side up, and trace. Transfer design lines. (This will be the front.) Baste around outside seam (pencil) line to transfer seam line to wrong side.

On *wrong* side of second orange square, place sun template, right side up, and trace. Transfer face *circle* only. (This will be the back.) Baste directly over circle to transfer seam line to right side of fabric.

3. On front square, add embroidery lines for face (do not embroider circle). Use black for eye pupils and yellow-gold for all other lines.

4. To make a front unit, stack front on a plain orange square, right sides together. Machine-stitch around outside seam line; do not leave an opening. Remove basting.

Repeat with back to make a back unit.

Turn each unit over (plain side up) and mark a cross in the center with 2″-long lines. Pull top fabric up to separate layers, and carefully cut along lines of cross. (This opening will be used to turn units right side out.)

5. Add batting. Place each unit, cut side up, over a layer of batting and machine-stitch directly over outside seam line.

Trim batting to seam line. Cut out fabric around sun, leaving just under ¼″ for seam allowance. Clip into V areas and inside curves, and trim corners.

6. Turn each unit, through cut

lines, to right side. Work seam to edge and press lightly.

7. By machine, and using matching thread, topstitch around circle on both front and back units.

8. Place front unit on top of back unit, cut sides together, with sunrays of back showing through sunrays of front. Pin together along circle.

To mark opening for dowel, place a pin on circle directly under center of nose. With two more pins, mark ¼" to each side of the center point on circle; this ½" will be left open.

Fold sunrays out of way and begin hand-stitching units together around circle. Catch inside layers only, and stuff circle between units with fiberfill as you go; leave ½" open at bottom for dowel.

9. Glue sun to dowel; see *To make a stuffed ornament*, Step 5, page 113.

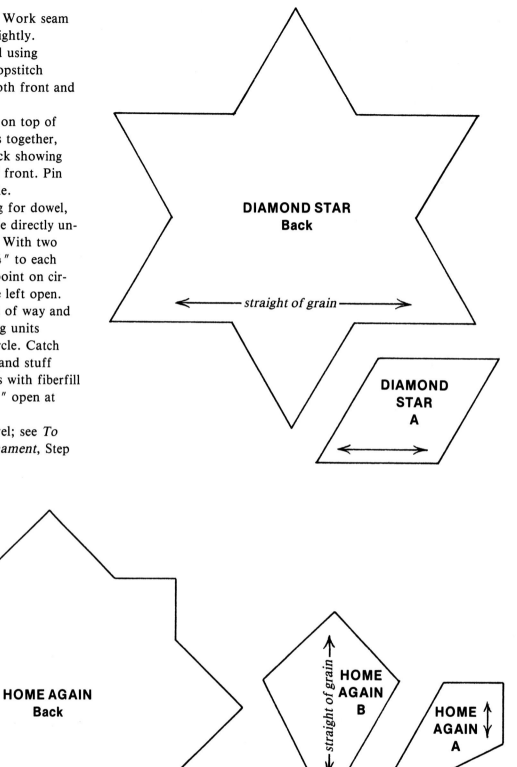

DIAMOND STAR
Back

← *straight of grain* →

DIAMOND STAR A

←→

HOME AGAIN
Back

← *straight of grain* →

HOME AGAIN B

↕ *straight of grain*

HOME AGAIN A

↕

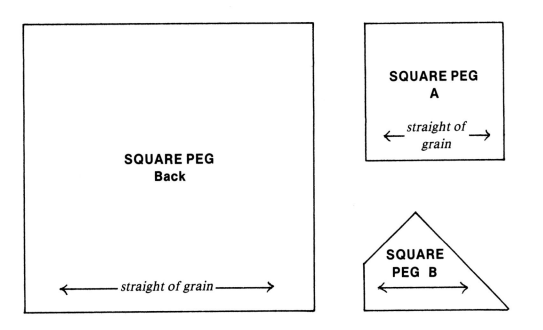

SQUARE PEG
Back

straight of grain

SQUARE PEG
A

straight of grain

SQUARE
PEG B

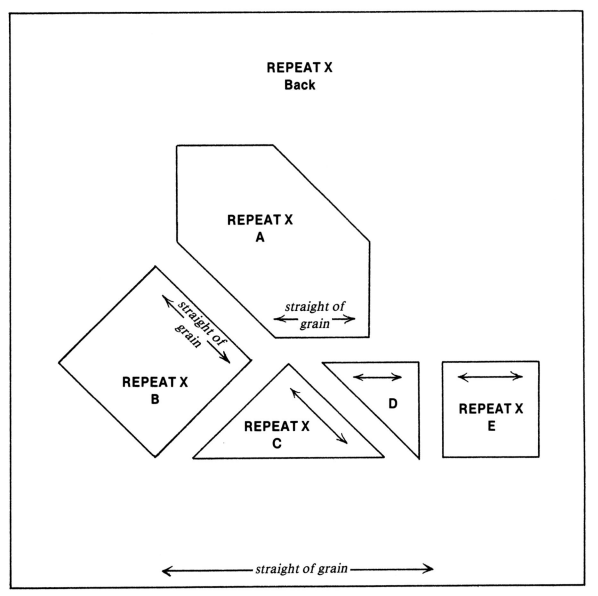

REPEAT X
Back

REPEAT X
A

straight of grain

REPEAT X
B

straight of grain

REPEAT X
C

D

REPEAT X
E

straight of grain

short broken lines are embroidery lines

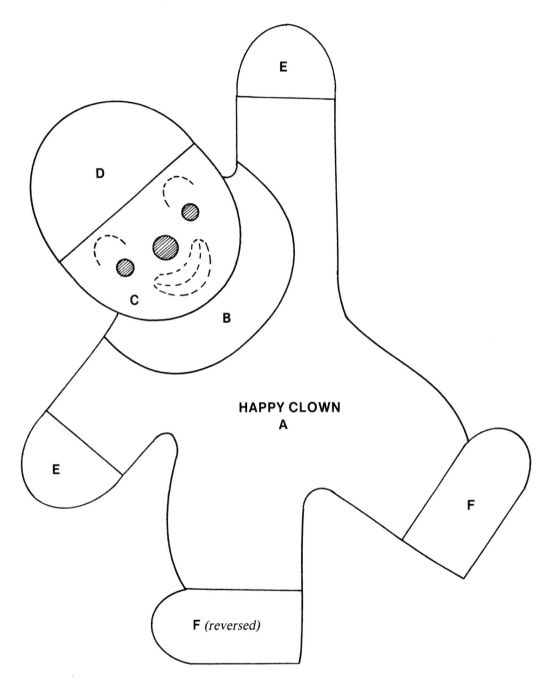

HAPPY CLOWN
A

short broken lines are embroidery lines

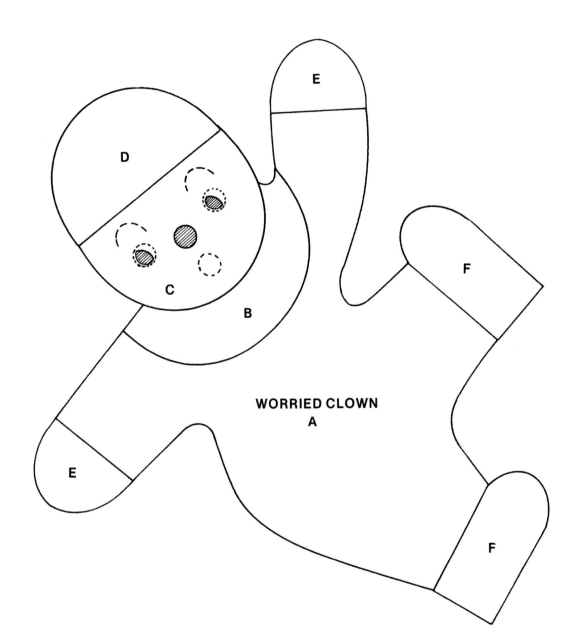

WORRIED CLOWN
A

short broken lines are embroidery lines

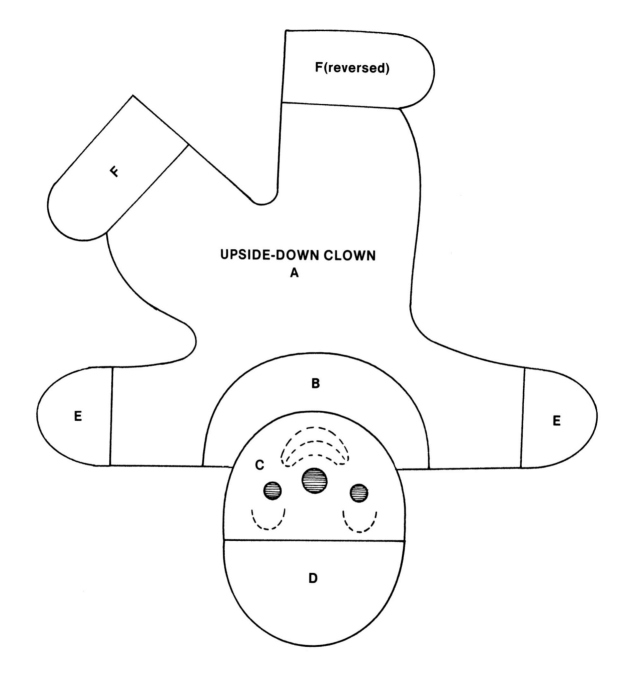

short broken lines are embroidery lines

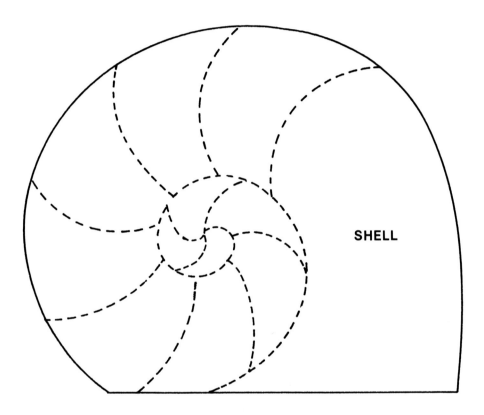

SHELL

Index

Names of patterns are in capital letters
Page numbers for photos are in boldface type